"Powerfully convincing . . . could help to change corporate cultures . . . a vastly important, necessary change to the way we do business . . . if I could, I would make it mandatory reading for executives."

LYNNE B. HARE
Program director
Kraft Foods

"A must-read book for all business starters, managers, supervisors, and owners . . . a wonderful, much-needed book."

GABRIELE PILLMAN
Associate quality engineer
Ergotron

"Relevant . . . an excellent and timely message. . . . I know from personal experience that employees are more valuable . . . than all the assets on the balance sheet. . . . I am in total agreement."

VICTOR E. SOWER, PH.D., CQE
Professor of management
Sam Houston State University

"Forthright and refreshing . . . well-written . . . easy to read . . . a valuable self-improvement tool."

L. DAVID WELLER
Professor emeritus of educational leadership
University of Georgia

Managing with Conscience for Competitive Advantage

Also Available from ASQ Quality Press:

Bringing Business Ethics to Life: Achieving Corporate Social Responsibility
Bjørn Andersen

Transformational Leadership: Creating Organizations of Meaning
Stephen Hacker and Tammy Roberts

The Trust Imperative: Performance Improvement Through Productive Relationships
Stephen Hacker and Marsha Willard

Making Change Work: Practical Tools for Overcoming Human Resistance to Change
Brien Palmer

The Synergy of One: Creating High-Performing Sustainable Organizations through Integrated Performance Leadership
Michael J. Dreikorn

Finding the Leader in You: A Practical Guide to Expanding Your Leadership Skills
Anton G. Camarota

Office Kaizen: Transforming Office Operations into a Strategic Competitive Advantage
William Lareau

Observations from the Trenches
David H. Treichler

To request a complimentary catalog of ASQ Quality Press publications, call 800-248-1946, or visit our Web site at http://qualitypress.asq.org.

Managing with Conscience for Competitive Advantage

Pete Geissler

ASQ Quality Press
Milwaukee, Wisconsin

American Society for Quality, Quality Press, Milwaukee 53203

© 2005 by American Society for Quality

All rights reserved. Published 2004

Printed in the United States of America

12 11 10 09 08 07 06 05 04 03   5 4 3 2 1

Library of Congress Cataloging-in-Publication Data

Geissler, Pete, 1933–

    Managing with conscience for competitive advantage / Pete Geissler.

      p. cm.

    Includes bibliographical references.

    ISBN 0-87389-638-6 (alk. paper)

    1. Business ethics.   2. Industrial management—Moral and ethical

    aspects.   3. Organizational behavior—Moral and ethical aspects.

    4.   Social responsibility of business.   5. Trust. I. Title.

HF5387.G445 2004

174'.4—dc22   2004015940

ISBN 0-87389-638-6

Publisher: William A. Tony

Acquisitions Editor: Annemieke Hytinen

Project Editor: Paul O'Mara

Production Administrator: Randall Benson

Special Marketing Representative: David Luth

ASQ Mission: The American Society for Quality advances individual, organizational, and community excellence worldwide through learning, quality improvement, and knowledge exchange.

Attention Bookstores, Wholesalers, Schools, and Corporations: ASQ Quality Press books, videotapes, audiotapes, and software are available at quantity discounts with bulk purchases for business, educational, or instructional use. For information, please contact ASQ Quality Press at 800-248-1946, or write to ASQ Quality Press, P.O. Box 3005, Milwaukee, WI 53201-3005.

Quality Press
600 N. Plankinton Avenue
Milwaukee, Wisconsin 53203
Call toll free 800-248-1946
Fax 414-272-1734
www.asq.org
http://qualitypress.asq.org
http://standardsgroup.asq.org
E-mail: authors@asq.org

AMERICAN SOCIETY
FOR QUALITY™

To place orders or to request a free copy of the ASQ Quality Press Publications Catalog, including ASQ membership information, call 800-248-1946. Visit our Web site at www.asq.org or http://qualitypress.asq.org.

∞ Printed on acid-free paper

CONTENTS

PREFACE: THE VIRTUES OF MANAGING WITH CONSCIENCE

Employees and customers are more than every business's "most important assets"; they are the assets from which all others radiate.

I doubt that anybody in business of any sort or size could have missed reading the inflammatory headlines and sordid tales of corporate malfeasance and demise that have sensationalized the business press since the mid-1990s. Enron's shady and covert financial manipulations to hide big losses, raise the price of its stock, and enrich its top executives—followed by its bankruptcy—perhaps made the loudest splash. Tyco followed suit, with its top guns—two of whom are being tried for fraud as I write this—justifying huge bonuses and expenditures for artwork charged to the company. The nepotism and outright fraud at Adelphia led to the arrest of the patriarch and his two sons, each of whom skimmed millions from the company's coffers. And Westinghouse, a company with a household name and a long and enviable string of technological "firsts" that added greatly to our way of life, was mismanaged to a fire sale of its assets, but not before the scoundrels in charge fled with huge bonuses and pensions. The company's virtual demise—a few scattered remnants still exist—severely harmed the city of Pittsburgh and dozens of other cities and towns in which it operated, and, literally, countless lives.[1]

We could point to many causes of these and other failures, and many of them would be gross rationalizations. For example, a former executive of one fallen company I know well is convinced that the company went belly up because of onerous government regulations. He has conveniently forgotten that other similar companies are still living happily within those same regulations, and he has conveniently forgotten the culture of greed and arrogance at the top, perhaps because a number of his friends were part of it.

The root cause of many failures, however, seems to be that familiar goblin: managing too zealously for stockholder value (or for an incessant drive for short-term profits or "profitable growth," which is a euphemism for the same misguided—dare I say conscienceless?—mission of management). I never liked that mission for all sorts of reasons, but mainly because it serves top managers more than any other group. (I and, I think, a growing number of people interested in business and its image actually consider managing for stockholder value to be amoral and a cruel hoax. We have become convinced that too many self-serving, short-sighted and, as a consequence, destructive decisions are made in the name of stockholder value—a conviction that is tackled peripherally throughout this book.)

Early in 2004 the Harvard Business School agreed tacitly that managing for stockholder value is amoral: it started a semester-long course in ethics for its MBA students. In announcing the course, the dean said, reportedly with a shocked demeanor as if this revelation was brand new: "An unsettling number of business leaders apparently have put their own motives and profit before integrity." The University of Maryland has taken a different approach to the same subject; its business students tour prisons and interview white-collar criminals in an effort to scare them—the students, not the inmates—into some sense of Conscience.[2]

Perhaps not so strangely, the chairman of a giant manufacturer of electronic equipment said, after his predecessor's attempts at managing for stockholder value had failed and the stock price of his company dropped more than 80 percent, that "stock price is a byproduct (of good management); stock price isn't a driver. And any time I've seen any of us (presumably top managers) lose sight of that, it has always been a painful experience."[3] I wonder if he feels the pain of the thousands of smaller investors who lost their shirts before he came to this revelation.

Strange, isn't it, that the "stakeholders" that must be classified as "big losers" to the mission of stockholder value are the millions of smaller investors—including lower-level employees—who were supposed to benefit. Spoon-fed operating statements and balance sheets that have been spun drastically—witness the Enron debacle—those investors didn't sell in time to miss the meltdown.

Other big losers are the towns and cities in which these companies operated, and all the local support businesses and their employees . . . customers who were forced to find other suppliers . . . employees who were forced to find other jobs and careers.

A former top executive at Westinghouse (one of the very good managers who was "fired" because he tried to infuse some integrity into the company) asked me rhetorically how many millions of lives were disrupted or ruined because of the company's—management's—failure . . . how many divorces, lost college educations, postponed or canceled retirements, resulted. I replied that I could think of at least a dozen such upsets in my small circle of friends. He could think of hundreds. "Millions" of personal trials and disasters is not hype by any means, and this from one of the smaller and less-publicized incidents, and perhaps one that showed the way for others. He then asked me to write a book entirely about these personal tragedies. "Management needs to know the results of its actions on the human condition," he mused. "You mean they don't know?" I asked with great disbelief. "I think that most managers, especially in larger companies, are so insulated from workers and communities that they don't have the foggiest idea of basic human suffering," he replied. Ouch.[4]

A middle manager from PPG who was "downsized"—in this case a euphemism for "replaced by a younger person who will work for a lower salary"—also suggested that I write an entire book on broken lives. "There are millions of us out there," he said, "and managers need to know the consequences of their actions, and how we feel about them."

Purpose: A New Direction. A New Way to Think about Assets. A New Attitude toward People

I do not intend to write another screed about the greed, self-centeredness, and self-aggrandizement of managers, who, to their everlasting discredit, perpetrated and profited from the failures of their companies. The journalists of the world have told, and are continuing to tell, that sordid story quite nicely without my help. (And every time they unearth a new scandal it seems that they also call for more regulations, as if they would prevent additional scandals. Regulations won't—a new Conscience infused with compassion and respect for people will.)

My purpose is, at the very least, to suggest a management direction that could prevent more of the same failings. The suggested direction could, I hope, restore a sense of social consciousness to management that, the headlines tell us, seems so lacking. (The consensus of those managers who have contributed to this book is that many of their peers, particularly in smaller organizations, already are guided by the new direction, just as they are. They also lament that all managers do not follow suit simply because it seems so simple, successful, and humane.)

To that end of a more universal acceptance, I suggest this new direction that is the best of all worlds: profits that raise stock prices, plus continuity of the business that benefits society as a whole. The new direction recognizes clearly that *every asset of every business—yes, every one—is a product of the two assets that aren't mentioned on any balance sheet or operating statement—employees and customers.*

OK, they aren't really assets in the sense that stockholders own them or that banks have used them for collateral against loans.[5] But nobody can deny that they are assets nevertheless. In fact, many annual reports and speeches by executives affirm that employees and customers are the company's "most important assets."

The two assets are irretrievably joined at the brain in the tightest of mutual dependencies. Customer satisfaction—and its close relative, competitive advantage—is a product of employees who work toward that end; all the managers who have contributed to this book know that intuitively. Without employees, customers couldn't be satisfied, and business—repeat business, too, and perhaps especially—would dry up. And, in a never-ending circle of basic truths, without customers, there'd be no need for employees.

I fleshed out the idea that employees and customers are the sources of all other assets (not the only assets, the sources, the mother lode) and ran my eyes down the balance sheets in several annual reports.

Factories, buildings, machinery, and equipment—all the tangible assets—all spring directly from customers who pay for products and services. No customers, no tangible assets. Simple.

Patents, copyrights, research, product knowledge—the intangible assets, the so-called intellectual property—are all in the heads of employees, not file cabinets or computer memories. Lose those employees, lose the business. (My small business is the perfect example, as you'll see in Chapter 7. If what's in my head is lost, the business is lost as well.)

I moved to the operating statement—revenues, profits, salaries, and dividends—all directly from customers. I paused at "working capital." Perhaps I could argue that capital—especially initial capital—emanates from the financial markets, including banks and investors of whatever stripes. The counterargument would be that the markets are eager to fund a startup business that is based on a good idea—which of course is held in the head of one or a group of employees. Can you name a business that wasn't started with an idea?

The markets are equally eager to finance a going concern with a positive cash flow, a result of customers who send checks. So perhaps it's not a stretch to say that capitalism itself is based on employees and customers! Was that what Peter Drucker had in mind when he reminded us that the first legitimate purpose of every business is to find and serve a customer? And could he have completed the thought by adding: "and the employees needed to meet that purpose"?

If the Concept Is So Simple . . .

My conclusions: First, that the two "major" assets of any business are employees and customers, and all other assets are "minor" in that they fall out from the major. And second, that all businesses should be managed for the "satisfaction" of employees and customers. Simple, but . . .

Many businesses I know appear to be managed for dissatisfaction of both. Consider . . .

Customer service is now often the responsibility of the customer. Customers pump their own gas, wash their own windshields, and check their own oil (mocking the outmoded term "service station" and replacing it with "self-service station"). We customers wade through tedious "menus" on the phone to get to other menus ad nauseam in an irritating effort to solve our own problems or buy a product or make an appointment, and so on.

Surprisingly, companies and individuals in service businesses seem to be leading the way in this draconian form of dissatisfaction. For example, calling my group of five doctors drops me into the never-never land of a long menu, wasting my time with irrelevance. My accountant's two-person business is even worse. The menu rarely relates to my needs, so I am forced to hang on the line to the long-winded end of its harangue, when a real person picks up; why didn't the menu offer the option to go there directly, or why didn't she pick up first? (I know, follow the money, and nuts to the caller.) The company from which I bought my computer is legendary for menus designed to be understood only by the techies of the world, a label that will never apply to me or to the millions like me, so we are second-class customers. I could go on and on, and, alas, you no doubt can come up with dozens of examples that irritate more than satisfy. They all make it harder and more infuriating to do business.

I know employees of firms large and small who gripe constantly about their jobs, again ad nauseam. My clients are good examples. The most favorable—and decidedly backhanded—comment I've heard for the past 10 years was, "If I must work, this is as good a place as any." Not much satisfaction in that kind of resignation. My best client complains loudly and frequently that his company is wildly dysfunctional, his word for the mountains of paperwork, almost all of it related to costs, he needs to complete before he has time to think about and do his real job, the one by which his performance is measured. And, by the way, he complains loudly that he doesn't have time to think, he is so immersed in paperwork. When he slips into that mode, I ask him, "What else are you being paid to do? Isn't your only job to think?" He doesn't have time to think of an answer, or even to see the irony.

His high-tech company, with annual sales of almost $2.5 billion, adds to the irony with its Help Desk, an employee-only internal website. Designed to "make it easy"—that's what the brochure says—to find and understand the inner workings of pension plans, health insurance, and the like, it actually adds to employees' frustration and anger by confronting them with a long and convoluted menu that prompts most to hang up, unfulfilled. Finding a human with helpful information is, in fact, not on the menu. Nobody is behind the desk.

At a local department store recently the salesclerk struggled with the cash register and apologized, "We were given new cash registers but weren't trained to use them, so I'm sorry for the delay." "Why do you want to apologize for bad management?" I asked. She replied, "Because I can think that, not say it." And I've written many speeches for top managers who recite, explicitly or implicitly, that tired cliché, "Employees (or customers) are our most important assets." Then, a short time later, the company—never the manager by name—announces it will "downsize" or "rightsize" or no longer serve a market that "doesn't fit" with the company's strategy for growth of revenue or profits. Am I the only one to see the hypocrisy and the dissatisfaction it unleashes on employees and customers alike?

Not long ago I wrote a speech for the CEO of a Dow 30 manufacturer with sales in the area of $12 billion. The audience was some 2,000 executives of a customer group that the company had served for a century and who contributed at least 30 percent of the company's revenue and a slightly lesser percentage of profits. The essence of the message was that the manufacturer would no longer serve this group because prices and profits were too low and the CEO had better places to invest. Everybody in the room knew what this shortsighted CEO really meant was, simply, "There are better places to raise the value of my stock options." The audience laughed, silently to be polite, and proceeded to purchase from the several competitors both here and abroad. That manufacturer is no longer in business, and the CEO, when I met him a few years later at a cocktail party, defended his moves as "good for the city, good for investors." I wonder how this man, obviously on Planet Denial, could find "good" in disrupting the lives of, literally, millions of loyal employees, customers, suppliers, and investors.

This Book Is about Possibilities

This book examines, first, the significant differences between managing with Conscience, the capstone of which is managing for the satisfaction of employees and customers, and managing for stockholder value. Then the book profiles a number of successful companies that are managed with Conscience, albeit in different styles. The managers of those firms invariably ignore short-term accounting figures; they know that their businesses are much more than numbers and behave accordingly.

The evidence in favor of managing with Conscience is necessarily anecdotal; the best accounting minds and practices cannot create before-and-after scenarios with any validity. So you who are looking for the quantifiable data of operating statements and balance sheets to validate the premise won't find it. Nevertheless, the experiences of the several contributors support what we like to call "conventional wisdom" and what the lawyers call "truth on its face." Perhaps I can call on our nation's founders for further support: "We hold these truths to be self-evident."

Greetings from the author. What a wonderful trip I've been on since I launched this project during the late fall of 2003. I've been wildly fortunate in finding managers in a variety of businesses who actually—and in defiance of the fear mongers in the media—walk the talk of managing with Conscience. They are totally convinced that Conscience is the root cause of respectable (not excessive, or, in the pejorative sense so loved by the media, obscene) profitability and that continuity of the business and the lives it supports is the real goal.

Jim Browne of Allegheny Financial—you'll meet him in Chapter 2—told me this would happen, and I bow to his superior prescience. What he didn't tell me was that I'd make a number of new friends along the way, and for that I am eternally grateful.

If perchance I am ever reincarnated and need a job, I want it to be with one of my contributors. You'll know why after you've read further.

1

THE INVISIBLE CHASM THAT SEPARATES MANAGEMENT STYLES

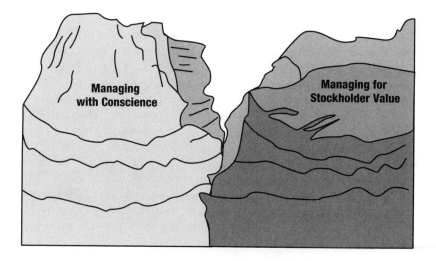

*Managing for stockholder value shares very little
common ground with managing with Conscience.*

I learned long ago that universal truths and clear-cut answers are rare, if not nonexistent. Therefore, managing with Conscience, which can be thought of as managing for the satisfaction of employees and customers, as the "point" or "overreaching" strategy may not be for every manager, every company. That said, I am quick to point out that *no* management philosophy or style is an island unto itself; each is surely tempered by any number of ancillary or supporting considerations that are beyond the scope of this book. Balance—and how managers tip the balance—is the name of the game.

For example, I know of one company that tipped the balance so steeply toward Conscience that managers neglected to invest in upgrading a major product line. The company slid from first to third place in the market, sales and profits plummeted, and a new management team is fighting to keep the company in business.

I can say that *tipping the balance* toward Conscience works very well for many firms in and out of my circle, as the profiles in the book demonstrate. The other side of that same coin is that tipping too far toward managing for stockholder value—which I'll shorten to Stock—has been destructive to many of the companies that practice it (or did for those no longer with us). Also destroyed or disrupted are the stockholders it supposedly benefits, and stakeholders such as employees, customers, suppliers, and residents of communities in which the company operates. Damaged or destroyed as well are the reputations of businesspeople who worked for those companies—including those who were not involved directly in some of the debacles but who became "guilty" by association. If high tides lift all boats, low tides drop all of those same boats. (I asked a former high-level executive of a "disgraced" company to write a review of this book so that I could quote him. He refused: "My obvious tie to this company would harm sales and credibility of the book, not help.")

Writing this book has confirmed to me that many positive and constructive results drop out of a tilt toward Conscience, and little positive or constructive out of a bias toward Stock. Some specifics:

1. **Conscience encourages long-term, strategic thinking and behavior**—which is espoused and applauded by every manager I know—for several reasons. Perhaps the first—and most elusive—is that it's very difficult to think short-term when the very lives and lifestyles of people are considered, unless, of course, managers can't muster any empathy for their fellows. One interesting corollary is that empathic managers create meaningful, interest-

ing jobs that involve employees in the welfare and future of the business. You'll find impressive examples of this throughout this book. Another is that monthly or quarterly operating statements are either ignored completely or given a gratuitous glance.

The "bottom line" for these managers is zero to little turnover of employees and customers, highest product quality, and the lower costs and higher profits that they are convinced will surely result.

Stock, on the other hand, encourages short-term thinking and behavior; it gives executives draconian incentives to inflate stock prices to raise their options' value, to avoid considering anything but pecuniary gain. Decisions are made that inflate revenues and profits; witness Enron and Arthur Andersen, and, in my direct experience, Westinghouse. Plant managers at Westinghouse—and, I'm told, at many other manufacturers— would routinely ship product at the end of a month and before it was ready because, in the misguided and misleading accounting system in place, the revenue and profit expected from that shipment could be booked as soon as the truck or railroad car left the shipping dock. Immediate beneficiaries of this grotesque and self-serving form of mendacity were plant managers. They avoided embarrassing questions sure to be asked at monthly meetings to review P+L statements, pre-served their bonuses and reputations for at least until the numbers caught up to reality (or they could be promoted before reality caught up with them), and kept the CEO smiling as he reported glowing numbers to stockholders and analysts and watched the value of his options increase.

John Cassidy, in his article "The Greed Cycle" in the *New Yorker* of September 23, 2002, wrote, "stock options . . . give senior man-agers a strong incentive to mislead investors about the true condition of their companies."

The big losers, of course, are customers, who are invariably unhappy with partial shipments or shoddy products, and employees, who see the hypocrisy of managers who preach quality and customer satisfaction—which of course are birds in the same nest—and then ignore both.

A friend, a brilliant engineer who rose to one rung below the very top of a huge engineering/construction company, fell into an analogous trap. Under extreme pressure to grow—pressure applied by an overly ambitious CEO brought in from outside the company by an equally ambitious board—my friend negotiated (actually, "bought") projects valued at hundreds of millions of dollars, knowing full well that the contract prices were so low that the company could not possibly book the profits projected. My friend figured he'd "make it up with the extras," a risky but occasional "strategy" in construction.

The euphoria of booking big contracts led, in a few years, to the desperation of saving the company, and then to bankruptcy and the disappearance of yet another corporate icon.

The New York Times of February 7, 2004, in an article titled "Survey Finds Profit Pressure Leading to Poor Decisions," cited a study by Duke University and the University of Washington that concluded that "short-term often eclipses the long-term— more than half the companies surveyed said they would delay starting a project to meet their earnings target, even if they knew it to be profitable. About 80 percent said they would cut spending on research and development, advertising, or maintenance that would not hurt them in the short run but could hurt them over time—to meet quarterly earnings goals." Then, in some sort of perverse attempt to bestow some integrity onto management, the article stated, "*Only about* 10 percent of the companies surveyed said they would alter their accounting assumptions to meet a quarterly target, and *only about* 20 percent said they would postpone making an accounting change to meet a target." (The emphases are mine, because I would have written "an amazingly and disturbingly high percentage of the companies surveyed. . . .")

I was lunching with a director of marketing at Westinghouse and said, "Long-term planning at Westinghouse is deciding what to have during the next coffee break." "You have too long a view," he replied. "We work hard on strategic plans and then put the documents on a shelf to collect dust; then it's business as usual, minute by minute, fire by fire."

2. **Proponents of Conscience are concerned about costs,** as all managers should be. But, because of their longer-term thinking, they plan for the time when costs can be converted to revenue and profit. An example: Jim Browne at Allegheny Financial

Group doesn't expect certain new hires to contribute to revenue and profits for three to four years, and then expects stellar performance, and gets it, for many years afterward. And Ron Herring at MSA says that it takes 18 months for an employee to "get traction, and two years to really understand his or her job. We gladly take the short-term hit in anticipation of the long-term gain."

Stock, on the other hand, encourages cutting costs to raise profits and stock prices for the short term. In the long run, operating in that way actually costs big time, not only in money but also in bankruptcy. Ken Lovorn, in Chapter 9, tells of the president of a billion-dollar engineering company who managed by cutting heads when business was slow and then adding them when business improved. The costs to terminate and rehire were astronomical, especially in this cyclical business, and product quality suffered greatly as well. Which brings up a good point: strategic thinking requires faith that the future will be better or as good as the past, and cycles will level out. The same is true for investing.

3. **Satisfaction encourages win-win, team work, a culture of cooperation and equality.** Jim Browne's team (one member calls it "family" with perfect justification) is a stellar example: all four members share the profits and security of a successful business, and customers win with extraordinary service that extends well beyond money management. The whole team makes decisions, yet each member enjoys a strong autonomy. Frank, the enterprising bartender with a phenomenal memory who is the subject of Chapter 3, created, almost singlehandedly, a win-win culture in an entire hotel. And Kerotest, in Chapter 8, stipulates in its union contract that "if you can't work in a team, you can't work at Kerotest."

Stock, on the other hand, tends to create win-lose, a culture of adversity, extreme competitiveness, and divisiveness. Employees tend to do what is asked by bosses, rather than what is right for the business; the shipping policies at many companies are a good example. And a culture of divisiveness is common, although at times I wonder if employees know it in their eagerness to "buy in" to management's decrees.

I was lunching with a director of distribution (one short step below a vice president) at PPG Industries when he began to extol the virtues of Stock. I asked him if he thought it was fair for his boss and his boss's boss and so on up the chain to be rewarded with options for hundreds and thousands of shares of stock when his options were limited to fifty or a hundred shares. He stopped to think about that, I swear for the first time, before he answered that yes, it was fair, because those guys made more money than he did. I asked, very softly, if they were granted options at the same percentage of their salaries as he was granted, if they worked harder, longer, smarter than he did, and if they deserved their disproportionate rewards simply because of their broader span of control.[1] No answer. I wondered why this intelligent man had bought into a system of compensation that was, to me, so lopsided.

4. **Conscience encourages creativity, entrepreneurism.** The culture of Conscience encourages a free exchange of opinions, values, and thinking—not only among employees, but also among employees and customers. The cornerstone of Jim Browne's and Ron Herring's management style is *listen*—to customers first, because only then can employees understand customers' problems, needs, and wants, and then to other employees as minds mesh for creative solutions and services. And a cornerstone of Ken Lovorn's style is his customer advocate, whose job is to listen to customers—to look at every project and issue from the customer's point of view and then to be certain that employees doing the work understand it. I doubt if my friend with the construction company would have signed those losing contracts if he felt free to discuss what he was doing with the chairman or if he had listened to what his estimators were saying.

The stifling of creativity by Stock is amply illustrated by the engineering company that prompted Ken Lovorn in Chapter 9 to start his own shop. The high-level employees listening to the president were so intimidated—Ken wasn't—that they actually approved, by their silence, a strategy that was obviously misdirected. Yet I'm sure that each had a better way that at least could have saved the company.

5. **Conscience literally and inherently demands that customers receive more than they expect,** thereby creating the strongest possible competitive advantage and the highest possible percentage of repeat business (and lowest costs for sales and marketing). One of my clients asserts that "satisfaction" is too mild a concept for managers who understand its power; "delight" is more appropriate. Without exception, all of my clients have come to expect more than text from me; they also expect a hospitable environment that encourages creativity. All the contributors to this book have literally built their businesses around "doing more."

Stock, on the other hand, literally and inherently demands that the terms of contracts and agreements be met to the letter, or as close as possible. Anything more adds to immediate costs, and that is culturally unacceptable.

2

INVESTMENTS: NOT THE HALF OF IT FOR THIS FINANCIAL PLANNER

Listen: It's the profitable sound of success via satisfied employees and customers.

Jim Browne is the managing partner of Allegheny Financial Group, a financial services company that he helped found in the 1970s. He is also an interesting enigma. He devoted the first decades of his adult life to the priesthood, where he renounced all worldly goods and espoused religion. When he reached middle age, he left the priesthood to manage money for others and, along the way, to amass considerable money and other worldly goods for himself, his wife, and his children.

The group functions in three areas that are managed as separate entities to avoid conflicts of interest: financial planning,[1] private equity, and investment brokerage. With just under 200 employees, the group is the largest of its kind in western Pennsylvania. Its financial planning group—the focus of this success story—has been designated by *Worth* magazine as among the best managers in the nation.

Jim describes his planning business: "The ads we've run for years in various performing arts magazines here in Pittsburgh always describe our business in these terse words: 'Allegheny Financial provides asset management services for successful individuals, businesses and pension plans.' In fact, we do much more—we help customers enrich their present lives in all sorts of ways and plan their lives for the enriched future they envision. I purposely use the word 'enrich' because it implies money, of course, and much, much more. And I want to point out that the operative word is 'help'; we don't impose or dictate to people we think of as our partners. I'll flesh out these ideas later."

Our Value Is in Our Employees' and Customers' Minds

"We're a typical service business in that the value of our physical assets is virtually insignificant to our balance sheet or operating statement. Those assets include our equity in a small building that we own, and in the furniture, computers, and so on that we use every day.

"The value of our intangible assets is the inestimable value of our employees' and customers' minds. They are, in the truest sense, the company, and, of course, given today's accounting rules, they don't show up on any of our financial statements. Nevertheless, my partners and I know their value and behave accordingly.

"We agree that we operate our business with one umbrella principle: give customers more than they expect, and—the obvious corollary—hire employees who are able, intellectually and emotionally, to do that.

"Deciding how to give customers more than they expect is the easy part. Finding employees to do that is far more difficult and is our highest barrier, one that, despite our best efforts, we haven't yet learned to hurdle completely. Yes, we explain our philosophies during the initial interviews, and candidates nod and say that they understand and can work happily within them. Nevertheless, we see, far too often, some sense of discontentment replace the original sense of excitement during the first eight weeks of employment. That's followed by a sense that this relationship can't work, and either our new employee resigns or we ask him or her to go.

"I think that there is one central reason for this unfortunate chain of events—unfortunate financially and emotionally for both us and them. We are so focused on serving our customers beyond their expectations that I think sometimes that we have established a culture of servitude. I don't mean slavery—far from it—but servitude in the best sense of the English butler, the career, unobtrusive, behind-the-scenes, always-handy helper, supporter, confidant.

"So our employee turnover rate during the first eight weeks a new employee is on the job can be as high as 50 percent. After eight weeks it's close to zero; like any business we lose employees to death and retirement and sickness and changing family needs. But, unlike many businesses, we rarely lose people to dissatisfaction in any guise. One result is that our competitors know that raiding the company for talent is pretty futile and frustrating.

"'Employee satisfaction' is a three-legged stool: compensation, creativity, and involvement. We pay our people well, more than people in comparable jobs at other firms are paid, and our benefits are generous, including our profit-sharing plan.

"The second leg—creativity—is less obvious, less tangible, and less measurable; it goes by other, more descriptive names like 'stretching' or 'creative overload.'"

I asked one employee why he signed on with Allegheny Financial right out of college: "I think that the overall reason was the future Jim and others painted for me. I was offered training to become a certified financial planner—an important recognition of competency that is a prerequisite for success—and was told that I would be 'educated,' i.e., work in each of the three areas of the company to gain a broad view of the entire business and how it functions as a cooperative organism.

"Perhaps most important, I was told that I would not be expected to contribute to revenue until after my education was complete in three to four years. Jim, I know, is convinced that impatience for financial results can be counterproductive in that it can actually lose customers with products and services that fall short of standards. In essence, the company promised me a second college experience and a solid foundation of knowledge before exposing me to clients.

"I stay here because Jim knows exactly when and how far to 'stretch' me to expand my capabilities and keep me totally involved and interested in my job. For example, I immediately attended all sorts of meetings with clients and their accountants and lawyers, and I was put in charge of a limited partnership we formed, under Jim's wing, of course. That first partnership has been so successful that I was asked to form a second along the same lines and purposes. I am now one of the three General Partners that manage a growing portfolio.

"The bottom line is that I can see my business life 20, 30 years down the road, which has big advantages. I have, at age 28, a clear vision of my career path and what I need to do to be successful . . . all of which is vital as I work toward a partnership.

"To sum it up, I'm here for what the first President Bush called 'the vision thing.' The company and I share the same vision of my future, and we like what we see."

Jim Browne continued: "Involvement is also best explained by example. One long-standing client—who complains on the one hand that we overservice his modest account and on the other hand that he doesn't see enough of us because he enjoys our chats about our lives and the fresh insights he seems always to extract—is also a wine buff. He would object to 'connoisseur' as far too elevating and pompous, and in fact calls himself more of a wine snob. Anyway, he opens his house to me and the six others on my immediate staff—and that includes our receptionist—who help him be comfortable about his funds and life.

"He has told me repeatedly that managing his assets is only a small part of managing his comfort, his sense of well-being that allows him to focus on his own career and life and not on the inevitable ups and downs of the various financial markets. We gather twice a year or so for a lunch at his home that is really a reason for him to uncork and share his latest discoveries in his world of fine wines. My staff and I win with a clearer understanding of this client's thinking, a deeper empathy, if you will, of his needs that we can transfer, at least in part, to other clients. We all win with a good time."

The client responds: "When I retained Jim to manage my money I expected just that and no more. I underestimated him and his people right from the get-go of our relationship, when he asked me to answer some five pages of questions, in writing, about many other parts of my current life and how I envisioned my future. Answering those questions forced me to think more deeply and sensibly about what I was doing, and, perhaps more important, what I wanted to do down the road. Like many of us, I had vague notions about these things that I had not bothered to crystallize in any great detail, preferring to delude myself that I know on some intuitive level.

"'What make and model car do you drive?' was one question that puzzled me. Sure, my car counts as an asset of sorts, and, from that point of view, its value enters into any calculation of my net worth.

"That's not what Jim had in mind. When we sat down to review my answers, he stared into my eyes and said: 'You must understand that you are your most important asset; nothing in your portfolio of stocks and bonds, even your total portfolio, earns as much as you do. Even if we discount your earning power, consider that without you there is no reason for your stocks and bonds. So I want you to sell your car and buy a safer model.'

"'Now, there's an unexpected leap of logic,' I said.

"'Not so,' he replied. 'Your car ranks among the least safe on the road,' and he showed me the crash test results to prove it. He then gave me a list of safer cars and suggested that I work out a trade, which I did that week. Who could ignore advice like that?"

A Quiet, Revealing Conversation

Jim and his three assistants—Brandon, Carolyn, and Tara—met with me over lunch to discuss how their company fits within the framework and purpose of this book.

Brandon opened with some history: "Jim formed this team about five years ago and selected us very carefully for our sensitivity to clients' needs. The absolute key personal characteristic he was looking for is our ability to listen, and we think it's key to what I can only describe as our phenomenal growth."

Jim addressed me: "Pete, you've mentioned to me several times that the scarcest resource in business today is paying attention. We can't afford to *not* pay attention; we cannot plan and manage a client's finances unless we know that client, and I mean 'know' in ways that are far broader and deeper than his or her money. For example, how much risk is tolerable and how much can be spent on so-called personal assets. Both are basic personality traits."

At this point I noticed that everyone at the table looked intently at whoever was speaking and didn't say a word, and I thought how different we are than the people on the talk shows and meetings at other companies during which interrupting and "talking over" are so prevalent and annoying. How could anybody possibly hear, much less understand, what was being said?

"Our number one priority" said Carolyn, "is to provide clients with a service they can't find anywhere else, service that exceeds simply planning and managing portfolios. We literally become involved in almost every facet of our clients' lives, creating long-term relationships based on mutual trust and respect.

"One recent example: We were one of six firms being considered to manage the significant holdings of a wealthy family. When we won the account, I asked why and was told that the other five companies came to the first meeting with contracts all filled in and ready to be signed, which this person thought was pretty presumptuous. We came in with a blank pad and pencil and asked the right, probing questions, and then listened to the answers. They recognized that we were there to *learn* and then submit a proposal based on knowledge of their specific needs. We were the thoughtful supplier; they, the cookie cutter suppliers."

"Uncaring cookie cutters," interrupted Tara. "How can they care for a customer if they don't understand him or her? Impossible."

I chimed in. "I told you that you don't manage my money; you simplify my life by eliminating the chaos, the worries about my assets. I have much more time for myself now. I even gave up reading the *Wall Street Journal* for an hour every morning. My brain is clear of that kind of useless clutter."

"We want our clients to get more out of life, to do what they like to do and not fret over their money," added Brandon. "We simplify their lives in many ways, and maybe that's the key word: simplify. Look at your life, Pete. When you came here, almost 10 years ago, you were collecting at least 50 pieces of paper a month on all sorts of far-flung investments and you struggled to calculate your net worth and found it impossible to calculate yields. Now, we synthesize all that for you, and you can concentrate on your career and hobbies."

"I never could understand that phrase, 'It's not personal; it's just business,'" said Carolyn. "Our business is very personal; I put my personal touch to calls, e-mails, letters, and so on, and our clients recognize and appreciate it. So the personal approach helps us grow in countless, intangible ways. On top of that, it's just plain more fun for everyone."

"Our fee structure enters into the picture too," said Jim. "We might charge a flat yearly retainer or a percentage of assets under management, never a per-hour that nickels and dimes. As a result, clients are much more comfortable calling us with their concerns or for advice. Not one has abused that simple perk. And we try, via a thorough review, to cut the living expenses for each client by at least as much as our fee. In that way, our clients for all intents and purposes get our services for nothing.

"Here are a few examples. One client didn't realize that nursing home fees are tax deductible until we pointed that out to him. The savings were huge. We've lowered financing costs for several clients by restructuring debt, lowered medical insurance costs for another couple by pointing out that they were insuring their grown children who had their own policies and for another elderly couple who carried insurance for pregnancy when they were well beyond childbearing age."

Tara then pointed out services that are beyond the norm. "We found a deficiency in one client's liability coverage and showed another how to provide for a disabled child after the client's death." Tara chuckled: "One client literally came back from the grave to ask us for a favor. His will stipulated that his funeral be a major bash at his club, that we handle all the arrangements, and that Jim give a speech about the many happy and upbeat times in the client's life that we shared and loved. This person wanted his friends to celebrate, not mourn."

"I was flattered and flabbergasted at the same time," said Jim.

"It was a task equal to planning a midsize wedding," added Carolyn. "We pulled it off."

I thought back to when I sent my daughter to Jim for a consultation; she had just inherited about $40,000 and wanted to invest it prudently. This team did as thorough a life style analysis for her as they would have for a multimillion-dollar account. And charged nothing. I'm sure that my daughter and her husband won't forget this extraordinary service and will become clients when the time is right.

"OK," I said to Jim's three assistants, "what about you guys? What keeps you working at Allegheny? Brandon has already talked about his clear career path and his abilities being stretched."

Carolyn answered: "If I'm going to spend 8, 10 hours a day anywhere, I want to enjoy those hours. I do, and my attitude shows through to clients. To provide that higher level of service I mentioned earlier, you must enjoy giving it.

"I agree with Brandon about stretching; we're encouraged to think 'outside the box,' to come up with good ideas to improve ourselves and the business, and implement them. Management is very receptive, very approachable to new ideas. And I don't want to neglect the high standards of integrity and ethics set by our managers and partners, and that we naturally follow. I sleep well because of that."

"Let's not forget money," added Tara. "We are all well paid, so more is expected of us, which adds to the 'stretch' idea. I think all of us agree that we could not leave here without taking a major cut in both psychic and monetary pay; I know I couldn't."

3

THE BARTENDER AS ENTREPRENEUR

The sweetest words are a person's name,
"welcome back," and "the same."

Imet Frank eight years ago while attending a convention in D.C. Around three o'clock one slow afternoon I strolled into his bar (and "his" is the right word, as you'll see) in the small and upscale hotel in which I was staying, papers to be studied under my arm and a deep need for a stiff drink in my eyes. Frank—thin, trim, dressed in the traditional royal-red Eisenhower jacket over a starched white shirt and black bow tie—stopped polishing his wine glasses, already glistening, and asked me my pleasure. "Mart, rocks, dry, no fruit," I recited, as I slid onto a cushioned bar stool and glanced at the few fellow afternoon drinkers and an expensive lounge that I'd love to call my living room.

Our chat covered the usual idle banter that's endemic in most bars: Pittsburgh and why so many people think of it as bigger and dirtier than it is, what's right and wrong with the Steelers and Redskins, what I do for a living, how long he had been at his bar (decades, it turns out), why I was in D.C., our kids, and so on.

But I felt a big difference that told me that this was no ordinary barkeep. I realized that Frank really listened (paying attention is probably the rarest skill in business today, yet it can pay off handsomely, as was discussed in Chapter 2). He was really interested, and I found myself really listening and becoming interested in him; amazing how it always works that way. (Try it with your boss, significant other, and friends and reap the benefits.) Over two hours, we developed the kind of underlying rapport that I had experienced only with long-standing friends.

Or long-standing clients.

I returned to D.C. two years later for another version of the same convention, and I made it a point to stay in that same hotel. I again walked into the bar one slow afternoon. "Hi, Pete," Frank greeted me, "Welcome back. The usual?" and he made me my mart, rocks, dry, no fruit. We picked up our conversation as if we had never ended it, and I marveled that we did. After all, we both had met and talked with literally thousands of people since we had last met.

> Studies show that sales reps in places like department stores—and, presumably, bars and restaurants—who remember customers' names increase sales 239 percent over reps who do not remember customers' names. A touch on the arm can increase sales even more.

The story hasn't ended. Some four years later I went to D.C. to an opera and didn't think even once about booking another hotel even though my travel agent said that Frank's Place isn't at all convenient to the opera theater at Kennedy Center. Frank wasn't behind the bar—he died a year before, the new bartender told me. "But," he said, "he's here"—and he pointed to a brass plaque, "Frank's Bar," displayed prominently on the back wall. I told the interloper my story, and he chuckled: "I've heard dozens of stories like that, no two exactly alike. Frank recruited an army of friends who came back here time and time again. He treated customers like they should and want to be treated, and—you want to know something strange in today's world?—the hotel's managers knew it and counted up all that repeat business and treated him like a king. On top of that, they treat *all* of us like kings and queens, hoping to make us all Franks. This is the best hotel to work in anywhere, I'd guess, and it's all because of Frank."

My lady friend and I decided to dine that evening at the hotel restaurant, partly because it had recently been voted "most romantic dining spot" and partly because I wanted to learn more about Frank. What was it about him that compelled people like me, who know dozens of bartenders, to return time and again not only to his bar, but also to the hotel?

My waiter listened quietly to my little story of crossing paths with Frank and, without saying a word, disappeared into the kitchen and returned with the chef.

"Frank is the reason I'm here," the chef said after we were introduced. I asked for the story, and he sat down, suggested dinner and the right wine. "On the house," he said. "We'll celebrate his life."

"Frank had an amazing charisma, an amazing memory, and the two are inseparable," he said. "He never forgot a name or face or the story behind it. A mind like that—he could have been a chess champion.

"Anyway, he called me about five years ago and asked if I'd join him here. Told me he'd built a large group of steady customers who really appreciate fine dining and service. By that time his reputation was everywhere, so I agreed. Frank convinced the hotel's managers that we'd make a terrific team, and we did. This small dining room"—and he swung his arms in a wide circle that took in all 20 tables—"can't be beat for its friendliness, and, I like to think, for its fine food and drink. Business has been very good—profitable, and enjoyable, too, for us and for our customers."

I reflected during the drive back to Pittsburgh that Frank was a marvelous businessman; he intuitively understood the win-win behind successful relationships and was willing to make the effort to form and keep them. He won with a decades-long career that I'm sure paid handsomely in tips and friendships. His employers at the hotel won with an extraordinary amount of repeat business—I was the perfect example, and I was only one of hundreds, maybe thousands—not only for the bar and dining room, but also for rooms. Congratulations of the highest order to the managers of the hotel for recognizing Frank's contributions to the entire business. And other employees won with a role model who literally created—single-handedly—a great place to work that probably would be just another hotel if he had never been there. Quite a legacy.

There Are Other Franks in the World

Back in the 'burgh, I thought about the many bartenders and restaurant owners I know and why I return gleefully and often to some and not to others. I feel unusually well qualified to talk about this because I am somewhat of a social gadabout and am recognizable in the small cultural district of this small city.

Mark, an imposing figure behind the semicircular bar of an upscale restaurant in which he owns a piece, always greets me after a performance with, "Hi, Pete, wine or scotch tonight? What show did you see? Anything good?" and then, "I see that Duke is hot on the boards again this year. You'll be watching a lot of basketball." I see Mark at least twice a week, and his bar is usually packed two and three deep with people who are treated with the same jovial friendliness as I am.

John, around the corner at an equally upscale restaurant, always greets me with that tired, generic "What'll it be?" I asked him once why he doesn't address me by name; after all, I know his. His reply: "I'm good at remembering faces, not names." I see John maybe once a month, despite being almost always able to get a seat at his bar.

Craig owns the hottest jazz joint in town, and it's only a 10-minute walk from my house. He and his wife, Melissa, who works there off and on, *always* greet me by name, welcome me back, and ask about my daughter in New York (where their son lives) and when I'll be teaching again at Carnegie Mellon University (where their son was one of my students). Meanwhile, the bartender, who has been there for many years, has, without anyone saying a word, poured me a glass of my favorite wine and is warming it in her hands because she knows I like it with the chill off. And she always delivers it with, "Here, Pete, enjoy." It's not surprising that I hear a lot of jazz at Craig's place, and so do many other people who also enjoy his camaraderie. As I've said, it's one of the hottest spots in town.

Joe is manager of a local restaurant that is part of a small chain. He always greets me by name and asks if I want my usual wine or if I want to try a new variety. His bartenders and waitresses know not only my name but also the names of the several clients and friends who regularly join me there for lunch. In a neighborhood packed with restaurants, I go to Joe's most often.

Am I a sucker for friendliness that I know is offered for some commercial gain but I'm sure is sincere, too? You bet I am, and I love it. Don't we all?

And for you who think that what I've discussed in this chapter is "conventional wisdom," I ask: If it's so conventional, why is it so rare? And is it applicable to every business? You bet it is.

4

CEC: PROFITABLE GROWTH IN A CHANGING MARKET

Extraordinary focus on client and employee values is key to the rapid growth and stellar reputation of Civil and Environmental Consultants.

Jim Nairn is president and CEO of Civil and Environmental Consultants (CEC). "It's my turn in the box," he says jokingly of his firm's policy of changing management according to a written leadership and transition plan. He reflects on the story of their successful and progressive company:

"I want to start with some history, and how it led to how we manage our business. When we opened our doors as CEC in April 1989, the four founding shareholders knew that our first responsibility to ourselves and to any of the employees we hoped to have down the road was to grow, and the second was to assure that employees, not outsiders, own the company. We were young, in our 30s and early 40s, and had been employed by other consulting firms; we knew the opportunities and pitfalls. We knew then, just as we know now, that only growth opens new opportunities for employees—the opportunities of new challenges that encourage creativity and entrepreneurism, that keep us fresh.

"In our formative years we were growing so fast—if you looked at growth on a percentage basis—that we were doubling the number of employees every few months. Of course the rate of growth has slowed as we've become larger—we now employ more than 280 people, 130 here in headquarters, the others at our seven branch offices. We've grown an average of 20 percent per year during the 15 years we've been in business, and we've been named as one of western Pennsylvania's fastest growing companies by the *Pittsburgh Business Times* for at least a decade."

How to Grow in a Stagnant Market

"We're still growing despite being in markets that have been stagnant for at least five years. The reasons are quite basic. First, we know that our best customers now are our best customers in the future; we depend on them not only for repeat business but also for an increasingly larger share of their total business when that's possible and for referrals to other companies that can use our services. In that way, we are a bit like a stockbroker who wants to manage as much of each client's money as the client is comfortable having him manage and to be referred to other clients.

"Second, we are proactive marketers, never aggressive: we keep up with new products and changing policies or regulations, make our customers aware of these changes, and position ourselves to help our customers react to these changes, as necessary. Our suggestions demonstrate quietly that we're on top of the business and on top of customers' needs . . . an important marketing tool that has paid off.

"I think an important consideration for growth is our approach to marketing, specifically our sell-manage-do approach where our project managers sell the work and then manage and perform it. We employ one full-time marketing person in Pittsburgh and another in our Chicago branch—a very small staff for a company our size. A marketing coordinator who is responsible for providing things like brochures, press releases, proposal preparation, and periodic newsletters also supports the company.

"Our project managers bear the largest burden for marketing. They are responsible for securing new assignments, managing staff, budgeting client needs, and providing high-quality services. Their performance in these areas is reflected in their bonus compensation. The result is that best of all worlds: managers who sell and deliver a quality job on time and within budget, and a satisfied customer who has no reason to shop elsewhere."

The engineers to whom I teach writing invariably think that "sell" is the purpose of proposals, and "inform" the purpose of reports. They're right about proposals, wrong about reports since reports are the bridge to the next contract. A poor report—one that is murky, incomplete, or not reflective of the intelligence that went into the project—is far less likely to pave the way to the next project than a good report—one that is clear, concise, complete, and reflective of an understanding of the client's needs. Good project managers know that the primary purpose of both documents is to persuade, the secondary to inform.

Why Growth Is Important

Jim continued: "You might ask why such an emphasis on growth? The other side of growth is decline or stagnation. Without growth, where are the opportunities for our employees to grow within our system? Stagnation results in a lack of opportunities and forces your best employees to look elsewhere to achieve their professional goals. Stagnation is therefore unacceptable!

"The cost of hiring new employees is phenomenal, as everyone in business knows. The initial cost is high enough, but, frankly, it's small compared to having an employee on board who doesn't fit your culture. We've been fortunate to avoid stagnation and, for the most part, the pitfalls that it produces.

"I agree with other contributors to this book when they say that it doesn't cost anything to keep a customer; all we have to do is our jobs better than our competitors do theirs. In addition, our financial well-being depends on it: the cost of finding a new customer to replace one we've lost for whatever reason is at least 10 times the cost of keeping one. Again, we've been fortunate and have lost only one customer in 15 years in business. Many of our best customers have been with us since well before we started CEC when we were employed elsewhere."

Strategies for Growth

Jim laced the fingers of his hands, then continued: "Given that broad vision of growth, we've adopted three major, very related, and equally important strategies—I'd be hard pressed to place one as more important than the other: Having customers who appreciate our culture; nurturing our best employees, those who want to stay and build careers; and maintaining an orderly transition of management and ownership.

"Come to our company's picnics and other informal events and you'll see many of us wearing T-shirts that shout 'Client Focus.' It's more than a slogan here; we like to think of it as a way of life that is nurtured by how we're organized and operate. Unlike many of our competitors who are organized by discipline, we've been organized by client-focused groups since we opened our doors.

"I suppose that our guiding principle and privilege is to give each client more than expected, more than we promised, and every time I say or think that I'm reminded of the local butcher shop in my neighborhood. He stays in business despite the supermarket around the corner simply because he greets his customers by name and suggests a cut that fits their taste or asks about their children and grandchildren. He offers a personal touch that the supermarket abandoned long ago, but which many people still appreciate and are willing to pay a bit extra to enjoy.

"We give more than expected in a number of ways. Our managers, for example, are encouraged to become complete consultants. We train them to become our competitors, even encouraging them to become the main contact to a customer if that customer is comfortable with that manager. That transfer, by the way, is important: it's one way our employees grow into more responsible positions, become better consultants, and become more valuable to themselves, their clients, and to the company."

Jerry Dettore is the deputy executive director of the Urban Redevelopment Authority of Pittsburgh: "I've worked with Jim Nairn of CEC for more than 15 years, before he helped form CEC and became its president, and when I was an engineer here. I know that I can call Jim any time and discuss, say, the status of a project, and he'll know. He's involved all the way. I think of him as my project manager, although I know he depends on his actual project managers for the really fine details. Jim sets the tone, creates policy, is the de facto leader. And he knows how to work with the state and local offices of the Pennsylvania Department of Environmental Protection, saving us countless hours and frustrations of meandering through bureaucratic mazes.

"My staff and I work continuously with CEC, especially now that we are so deeply involved with a number of Brownfield projects during which we are always running into new challenges. Jim is quick to estimate the cost of the work, always conservatively; he rarely exceeds his estimate, saving me the many headaches of going back to my board for more money and explaining why. Several other suppliers tend to lowball costs to get the job and then 'make it up' with the extras. That always creates problems with budgets, and it almost always delays completion of the work.

"As a public agency, we are required to solicit bids for work and to award contracts to a broad range of suppliers. We try to work as much as possible with CEC, and it's easy to understand why. Perhaps it's a cliché to say this, but it's true: I can depend on them to think outside the box and come up with creative solutions. In short, CEC is the premier environmental consultant in this area, and they've earned our support."

"I was a client who became an employee," said Dan Szwed with a laugh. "For many years I was director of environmental affairs at Armco Steel, where my department was staffed to handle the 'normal' workload. When we were overloaded I called in outside consultants such as CEC. Over the years, Jim Nairn and I developed a strong friendship based on mutual respect.

"In May 1999 Armco was purchased by Kawasaki Steel, AK Steel was formed, and I was suddenly one of two directors of environmental affairs. I found myself contemplating future opportunities. Jim called an hour after the acquisition was announced and asked if I would be interested in joining CEC as a vice president and part owner. I was flattered, of course, and also curious about what I would bring to Jim's party. After all, I reasoned, I had never been a consultant unless I thought of myself as an 'internal consultant,' and I was management oriented, not task oriented as I know consultants must be.

"Jim explained that I would bring a customer's perspective, a kind of insider's insight, to the business, and that would be very valuable. He went further to say that my expertise in resolving the environmental problems of the steel and other metals businesses could expand that market niche for CEC, which fits the company's strategies for growth.

"I've been here for four years, and, I suppose because my experience as a customer is so ingrained, I still wonder if I'm a credible consultant. My friends and peers tell me that I'm the only person who wonders."

A "Best Place to Work"

Jim Nairn continued: "CEC was named one of Pennsylvania's best places to work in 2001. We didn't enter the competition in 2002 or 2003 simply because we were too busy; however, we plan to make the time to enter in 2004. The competition is sponsored by the Pennsylvania Chamber of Commerce, the *Central Pennsylvania Business Journal,* and others, and winning is a signal honor.

"My partners and I are more proud of that award than any other accomplishment during all my years in business, and I think it reflects the company's respect for employees and their respect for the company.

"Retaining key employees is critical in our business—a people business. Finding people who can sell-manage-do is getting tougher every year. Importantly, I can't remember when the last person above the assistant manager level left us. . . . I know that it was years ago, and he is now a manager at a big real estate developer, and a client.

"Good people stick with us for what we think are very good reasons. We think of our people—and our people think of themselves—as spokes in a wheel. Each spoke is essential if the wagon is to move; if one spoke breaks, the wheel and the wagon collapse, useless. It's our metaphor for teamwork, and it's our reason to treat employees as the valuable contributors they are.

"CEC provides substantial and generous benefits to all employees: health insurance, including coverage for prescription drugs; disability and life insurance; a matching 401(k) that is vested from day one of employment, which is very rare; a bonus plan that involves everybody from the janitor to the CEO; and tuition refunds for continuous learning. We then go the extra mile with our employee assistance plan—and with our employee stock ownership plan.

"I think that our deep concern for our employees is also very different from most firms in our business. Basically, we try to help employees and their families cope with all types of problems that affect their personal lives or job performance, and we do it without dwelling on what it says in the employee manual. In effect, what we do is spread the costs of extraordinary misfortune among all our employees."

"What's the headline about CEC from your point of view?" I was chatting with Marlene Harbert, human resources manager.

"Easy question," she replied. "The worst day here is better than the best day working anywhere else."

"Powerful stuff, especially coming from an HR pro. Tell me more."

"I'll never forget my two interviews to get this job, in 1999. Both were with the four founders. I could feel the camaraderie, the respect, the healthy joy of being here. We actually laughed almost the entire few hours we were together. I went home after the second interview and told my husband that I felt compelled to work for these guys. I figured that they treated employees that same way they treated each other. I was right."

"Do other employees feel the same way?"

"Judging by our turnover rate, I'd say so. Our rate is so low that we don't even measure it. I could if I had to, but what's the point? And, by the way, some 20 of our employees have been with the company since its founding 15 years ago, which is almost all of our employees who were with us then; the core of our genesis is still on board. Low turnover is great for growth, a connection that can be obscure to many managers. Say we lose an employee, a project manager. It costs at least three times that employee's salary to replace him or her, probably much more if you consider the loss of continuity with the clients, followed by the potential loss of repeat business. We also lose the respect of others in the industry—believe me, the word gets around when an employee leaves, and that can make it more difficult to hire new people."

"So you go the extra mile to keep your people?"

"Absolutely. Great benefits, as Jim has said, flexible hours and policies, and stability that's almost unheard of in consulting."

Jim continued: "I'm convinced that employees who own a piece of the action work more diligently toward growing the business than employees who don't have a stake. I suppose that that's conventional wisdom that bears repeating only because it's so important.

"I'm also convinced that it would be terribly selfish of the four founders, now in our 40s and 50s, to not transfer ownership to the next generation. As a result, all of our employees from assistant manager up participate in our stock ownership plan, which we started in the early '90s. Now, the original ownership group owns less than half the company, and that percentage is shrinking every year. Our managers buy more stock every year, with automatic withdrawals from their paychecks and a portion of their bonus as stock. Some of our managers now own 3 or 4 percent of the company, worth up to half a million dollars. The stock, by the way, kept increasing in value during the general market downturn during 2000–2003.

"The opposite side of the ownership coin is that selling stock in the company to outsiders isn't for us. Our growth by way of retaining good employees who are proud of their quality work that is completed on time and within budget, and customers who understand that, is the antithesis of what Wall Street wants and cares about: numbers, not people. So we decided even before we went into business to keep the company private. Besides, I honestly don't think that the consulting business fits the profile of a public company. The ROI can be impressive because the 'I' is so low, but the ROS isn't. In fact, it's pretty anemic when compared to, say, a well-run manufacturer or software developer."

Jim concluded: "I wish I could find a more descriptive word than 'relationship' to describe our extraordinary closeness to customers and employees. Perhaps 'culture' would be better. We assign a very high value to our culture, and it's working. We're still growing despite some flat markets, our employee and customer turnover rates are very close to zero, we rarely hire new employees except to accommodate our growth, and we haven't lost a customer in years. Also, most importantly, the next generation has bought into our culture and is poised to take over the business. Unlike many consulting firms, we have trained the next generation and they will be ready for 'their turn in the box' in the very near future."

5

MSA: SURROUNDING COMPETENCE WITH COMPETENCE

People want to work here; customers want to purchase here. There are reasons.

I slid the videotape out of its cardboard sleeve and out dropped a postcard with a dozen questions: Was the information presented in an interesting way? Presented clearly? Is the information useful? And so on. The card is a customer satisfaction survey that consumed maybe 30 seconds of my time to complete, and that is symptomatic of the customer focus at Mine Safety Appliances Company (MSA), the world's largest designer and maker of products that enhance the safety and health of workers throughout the world.

I found Ron Herring, vice president and general manager of MSA's Safety Products Division, the company's largest and most complex, through a column in the local newspaper titled *The Boss*. I knew that we are kindred souls when I read this secret to success: "You have to have fun doing your job." I express the same thought with "Make 'em smile" in Chapter 7. Then I read further and found that Ron's core values for success revolve around integrity, listening to customers and to employees, and working hard to satisfy their needs. I knew he was a "must do" for the book.

"People want to work here; they ask to work here," Ron said to open our discussion. "Our associate turnover rate is consistently below 1 percent and is lower than five other published indices, including Best Plants Practice, the bellwether. Most of the little turnover we experience is triggered by retirement or changing family circumstances, hardly ever to jump ship because of dissatisfaction. Oh, three or four associates left a few years ago to join the dot-com boom, which was an isolated incident. While we were disappointed in their decisions, at the end of the day it was their choice and we wished them well.

"Surely one reason our turnover rate is so low is our careful screening of applicants with team interviews, background checks, psychological tests, and so on . . . all to minimize the chance of error."

I probed: "Why do your associates want to stay here?"

"There are many reasons, of course. Topping the list is our business itself. We make products with a higher moral purpose: to protect the lives and well-being of those who use them. That may sound trite to the cynics of the world, but I assure you it isn't to our associates. In fact, it's so important that we call it the 'ultimate trust' and 'a passion to protect.' I think of those ideas as a combination of care and commitment, and it translates to people wanting to work here through pride, a sense of doing something valuable. They're the reasons I hear so often 'the best job I've ever had.'

"We are all reminded of that trust and passion by publicizing what we call 'saves,' specific incidents during which our products saved the health or life of a user. An example: First Sergeant Colin Rich's life was saved by MSA's MICH (Modular Integrated Communications Helmet), which deflected a bullet shot at the back of his head while he was on duty in Afghanistan. Sergeant Rich traveled 10,000 miles to the MSA plant in Newport, Vermont, where the helmets are made, to personally thank the associates there. The helmet exceeded its guarantee by deflecting a bullet three times bigger than the helmet is designed to deflect. He pointed to a hole in the back of his helmet: 'The bullet entered here, then took a right turn, bounced off my head, then skipped under the lip of the helmet.'"

An associate at one MSA plant said on the videotape I mentioned earlier, "My job is to protect firefighters' heads—I have several friends who are firefighters—I feel good that I helped save one from injury when some debris hit his helmet. I do the best job I can—won't let anything get out of here that can't do the job."

Ron continued: "Anthony Cruz, who works as a safety director for another company, literally saved his and his wife's lives by using one of our gas detectors. He and his wife awoke at 2 in the morning feeling lightheaded and nauseous. Anthony suspected carbon monoxide, retrieved his gas detector from his truck, and found that his suspicions were correct. He and his wife left the house and called the local firefighters, who located the source. 'I was able to celebrate a new year,' he remarked. The story is in our 2003 annual report.

"The second big reason associates want to work here is that they like being part of a successful organization, of being part of a legacy of success that is both financial and, if I can use such a broad term, social. One result is that we attract the best and brightest, and they form a critical mass of competency that grows on itself by attracting more of the same, setting in play a chain reaction in which every link is a winner."

"What about pay and benefits?"

"We do our best to keep our associates on board with both conventional and unusual policies. On the conventional side, our compensation package—pay and benefits such as health insurance and a 401(k)—is competitive and comfortable, in the midrange for our industry and area. Associates work here for steady and fair financial rewards.

"On the unusual side, we offer stability based on growing demand for our products since our founding in 1914, and a pleasant working environment that encourages creativity and self-actualization, and that features one of my top priorities: recognition for a job well done. We recognize individuals who have gone the extra mile via simple gestures such as gift certificates for family dinners, lunches with supervisors, and just plain 'thanks' from the boss.

"Any of our associates are eligible for monthly awards by living our values or making significant progress toward one of our goals. Clear demonstrations of the division's 10 core values are considered, including the less traditional 'have fun' and the more traditional integrity, quality, and teamwork. Entire teams that have meshed to arrive at extraordinary solutions to knotty problems are recognized as well."

"I know that you're big on teamwork. How do you decide who is on what team? What makes one team work better than another?"

"Our entire division is managed by team collaboration; I believe strongly that several sharp minds always arrive at better decisions than one.

"All of our teams are multidisciplinary, i.e., all affected disciplines are represented, whether the issue to be resolved is marketing, engineering, accounting—whatever. That makeup effectively eliminates functional silos, literally demanding that team members put their self-interests aside and look at how the issue at hand and its resolution affect the entire business.

"I see three characteristics of teams that are absolutely critical to their success and that influence our selection of members: mutual respect, sense of purpose, and sense of humor. Putting together a team without all three of these characteristics working together smoothly and synergistically is tantamount to sitting on a one-legged stool."

"Which brings us to sense of humor, or fun on the job. How do you encourage it? How do associates benefit?"

"Let's define 'fun on the job' first. I see it as doing what you like to do, which is almost always what you do best. We define it further in our operating plan as providing an environment that enables each other to grow, reach our full potential, and feel good about what we do.

"We try to encourage fun with family outings and other social events, some major, some minor. A group lunch, sending out for pizza, a gift of a ham or turkey, a family outing that is also an opportunity for spouses and children to learn about the business . . . those kinds of events or gestures add up to a sense of camaraderie.

"Fun is important. It's key to customer satisfaction, for example, because it shows in every communication and action, in something as subtle as tone of voice. Customers like to do business with people who are obviously upbeat and enjoying their work."

Carolyn, in Chapter 2, expressed the same thought: "Our business is very personal; I put my personal touch to calls, e-mails, letters, and so on, and our clients recognize and appreciate it. So the personal approach helps us grow in countless, intangible ways. On top of that, it's just plain more fun for everyone."

Ron continued: "Fun also raises productivity. Show me a worker with a smile and I'll show you a worker who is productive and is more promotable. So the company and its associates have a big stake in a simple idea.

"The flip side of that idea is a worker who gets up every morning and counts down the days to retirement. He or she drags down productivity and should move on to another job either here or somewhere else. Nobody wants to spend eight, 10 hours a day being unhappy, and nobody wants to be around an unhappy person."

"What about customer satisfaction?"

Eric Beck, director of marketing for the division, responded: "I could easily interpret the intent of all 10 of our core values to be customer satisfaction. But, as a marketing guy, maybe I'm a bit biased. Nevertheless, I know for sure that the main purpose of any business is to create and keep customers.

"We work toward meeting that purpose in many ways. For example, an intense Uncle Sam peers from posters throughout our offices and plants and asks: Who do you work for? The answer of course is every single one of our hundreds of thousands of customers: firefighters, construction workers, military personnel, plant workers—everybody worldwide who faces hazards on the job or at home, plus the distributors who sell to them. The answer is also in the first words on the video that we've already discussed: 'I work for First Sergeant Colin Rich.'

"Given that directed focus on customers, you won't find it surprising that our strategies include growth by providing products that exceed the expectations of customers, just as Sergeant Rich's helmet did. In addition, we are constantly working toward raising our customer satisfaction ratings via surveys and actions taken to rectify any deficiencies that the surveys uncover. As we've already seen, we go so far as to survey viewers of our videotapes, and make it easy for them to respond with valuable information.

"We also regularly monitor a number of what I call Listening Posts: our distributors, end-users, salespeople, customer service people, plant people, market researchers, the folks who track warranty costs—literally every group that is in contact with customers at any point in our supply chain. That encompasses just about everybody in the division.

"A multidisciplinary team sifts through what we hear and recommends actions. A good example: our distributors told us recently that they found it difficult to determine inventory levels of certain products. The committee examined our IT system, brought in distributors to demonstrate how they use it, and agreed that it is cumbersome. The system was revised not only to make it easier to determine inventories, but also to improve the flow of other information.

"Customers told us in another survey that our salespeople are tops in product knowledge and conveying that knowledge effectively, and that the quality of our products out of the box and over the longer term is the best in the business . . . it exceeds expectations.

On the other hand, we're not very innovative, the reason for the 'I' in DRIVE, our 2004 call to action that Ron will explain further.

"Each year we survey thousands of end-users and dozens of distributors to arrive at quantified customer satisfaction ratings. While the numbers are useful in planning our business, they could be more useful if we had them more frequently, more in 'real time.' We're working to achieve that. In the meantime, anecdotal evidence garnered from interviews with customers and the collective input of advisory councils made up of salespersons and other associates in close and regular contact with customers—plus the steady flow of orders that we enjoy—tell us that we're doing many things right."

> "How do your long-range plans support your focus on associates and customers?"

Ron continued: "Our plans include operating goals and the strategies and tactics needed to meet them. The written plans are accessible for reading by all associates everywhere. No exceptions.

"The plans are a careful balance of the social and financial values of our business. For example, the 2004 plan is called DRIVE for Excellence, with DRIVE expandable to: Delivery of what customers value; Recruitment and retention of associates who are caring, capable, and committed; Innovation in products and services; Value creation for shareholders via increasing returns; and Exceeding customers' expectations.

"We assign equal weight to each of those values, striving for a balance that assures equal treatment for all our stakeholders. Astute readers will note that four of the five values relate directly to associates and customers, which in no way implies that we think of profit as a second-class citizen. Profits are needed first to attract the investment needed to support employment and customers, allowing them to grow into new opportunities that are possible only when the business grows.

"Perhaps it's understandable that none of our eight actions for creating value mentions profits or profitability. What are mentioned are market opportunities, procurement strategies, alliances, brand recognition, and efficiency . . . all routes to profitability, just as our associates and customers are routes, not ends in themselves.

"I see my role, my primary obligation and the really creative and fun side of my job as a general manager, as dealing with and balancing the responsibilities we have toward associates, customers, the company, and the communities in which we operate."

Ron continued: "This business functions well because our associates subscribe fully to four overriding behavior patterns, all of which are difficult to define and learn, so we look for people who have them "built into" their personalities. The first is the willingness and ability to listen to each other and to customers. Only then can we understand and respond to everyone's needs. The second is to always act with integrity, which I define as always doing the right thing. I understand that 'right' is a matter for individual interpretation. I also understand that there are ethical standards to which we are all held, as we should be, and they are the standards. The third is the high energy needed to keep pace with a business that is constantly changing, growing, and demanding more creativity from each of us. And the fourth is that old standby fun. We're fortunate to have associates and customers who agree."

6

IT'S ALL ABOUT PEOPLE!

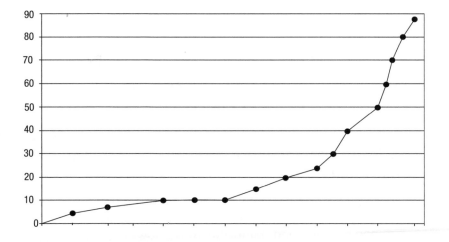

*This high-tech firm has been growing at
60 percent/year by living core values that center
on people and that never mention revenue or profit.*

The notion that growth of revenue and profit is the result of employee and customer satisfaction is clearly and unmistakably reflected in Vocollect, the global leader in voice-directed distribution.

"Management is all about people," said Roger Byford, chief technology officer, chairman, and one of the two founders of this high-tech firm. "Our core purpose is to create opportunity for all of us to grow and to excel in a fun and rewarding environment. That purpose stems from my past and the past of our other founder and protects our employees from falling into the same situation. We were both research scientists for a huge conglomerate, assigned to develop voice technology—the use of voice to enter data into a computer for such purposes as inventory control and other functions in warehouses. The commercial possibilities of the technology were too small for management to pay much attention to it or to fund it adequately. So my partner and I found ourselves in frustrating, dead-end jobs that we learned to dislike intensely. We wanted jobs without ceilings on our creativity and resourcefulness, and we wanted to offer similar jobs to others with similar feelings; we started Vocollect.

"Our five core values support the core purpose and are replete with such words as utmost integrity . . . team-oriented . . . friendly . . . individual initiative . . . creativity . . . intelligence . . . and balancing personal and professional lives."

"What about growth of revenue and profits?" I asked.

"Financial growth is important, of course, but isn't mentioned simply because it's a byproduct of good management, and, as I mentioned earlier, good management is all about people. Nevertheless, it's fundamental that no business can survive without the financial results that gladden the hearts of investors, but there's more to it than that. Growth also keeps employees happy by opening new opportunities to move to the next technical or commercial challenge—to develop the next generation of products that customers need, for example—or to move to the next rung up on the corporate ladder that wouldn't open up otherwise, and so on. The bottom line is that we owe it to our employees to grow so that *they* can."

"Several contributors to this book have talked about the importance of 'integrity' and 'do the right thing,' which are pretty abstract concepts. How do you define them, and how do you know that everyone in your organization lives them?"

"Integrity is, simply, what you see and hear is what you get. I could expand that by stating that you never want to do something that you wouldn't want to hear at your own funeral. That cliché encompasses honesty and much more, such as decency, trustworthiness, soundness, a certain openness that is reflected by a willingness to bare our business souls when appropriate.

"Here's an example: Our salespeople work directly with companies that operate their own warehouses, such as Wal-Mart and many of the grocery chains; they're the end-users of our products and services. They also work with companies that we call our 'partners,' for example, companies that sell material handling equipment to the same end-users. We want our partners to sell us as part of their package without feeling that we might go directly to the end-users, so we pay our salespeople the same commission for either type of sale, and we make sure that our partners know it. Our openness has worked: partners now account for 60 percent of our revenue, up from zero only three years ago."

"Let's talk about employees. What's your turnover rate, and why?"

Roger thought for a minute or two. "I can't remember when an engineer—the people for whom I am directly responsible as chief technology officer—has left us, and we now employ 70 of them. Turnover rate is so low, close to zero across the company regardless of responsibility or job title, that we don't track it. However, I'm not considering the occasional mis-hire who leaves, or is asked to leave, usually after only 90 days or so on the job. We've made a few mistakes on the front end of an employee's tenure and, when we realize that we have, we try very hard to find the right slot for that person. Sometimes we succeed; sometimes we don't.

"We revel in the benefits of low-to-no turnover—the far lower costs of hiring and training that are reflected directly on the bottom line, and the added time that we can devote to improving the business. We spend more time doing what we like to do and do best. Even more importantly, we benefit from the long-term personal relationships our employees build with our customers and partners.

"Why is our turnover rate so low? Because we live by our core purpose and values every day and in every way imaginable."

> "I see a huge need for communicating with employees and customers."

"Communicating with each other was easy when there were only a few of us; we all knew what we needed to know to function as an efficient organization with a defined mission simply by talking to each other and writing the occasional memo. Once we had more than 20 employees—looking back, it seems that 20 is the cutoff point—communications became a big problem, in some cases because we didn't communicate enough, but in others because we communicated too much. E-mail has made it too easy to transcend the barriers of 'need to know' to 'send it anyway to be sure all the bases are covered.' I'm sure that many organizations are afflicted with a similar overload.

"One of my current challenges, now that we employ nearly 200 people, is to find a way to slow down or prevent overcommunicating, which might require more communicating to employees to alert them of the situation—a Catch 22?—and to consider readers' needs more carefully.

"Clear and concise communications serve another purpose that we consider very important: they tend to stop political bickering, the backbiting and jockeying for position with the brass that I found so prevalent and distasteful with my previous employer. When everybody knows where everybody else stands, there's no need for this type of destructive behavior.

"As for our end-user and partner customers—there are more than 100 customer companies, no two exactly alike, and many more people within those companies—a core value is, again, 'do the right thing.' One right thing is to communicate with them on all levels, from top management to the folks on the warehouse floor who use our hardware and software.

"We keep in touch with customers via the usual personal visits, attending their trade shows, and advertising in their magazines. For example, we attend trade shows specifically for the grocery business, and we advertise in *Supermarket News,* among other magazines.

"Another example: I'm no longer directly involved in sales, but I still try to visit at least once a quarter with the people I know at Wal-Mart. And our service programs include regular site visits, on a 'whether you need them or not' basis, to let our support folks stay in close touch with the people using our products on a daily basis."

"Have you ever lost a customer?"

"Well, that depends on what you mean by 'lost.' We don't win every contract we bid on; it's unrealistic to expect to. Our sales model says we should expect to win one out of three: one of the other two is canceled, and the other is awarded to a competitor. Our hit rate is actually much higher, so our projections are conservative.

"But, we've never lost a customer once we've started to work together. I guess that's a customer satisfaction rate of 100 percent, and I'm proud of that. In that same vein, I'm very proud that many of our customers extend our original contract to other warehouses. For example, we are Wal-Mart's sole supplier of warehouse inventory systems—throughout the world. That's a particularly important achievement given Wal-Mart's well-known standards for efficiency and excellence for everything it buys."

"If I can summarize a bit, one reason that employees and customers are loyal to you is your core values. There must be others."

"Studies show that employees everywhere are loyal because of such characteristics of the organization as providing opportunities to do their best work and to grow into new responsibilities, recognition and respect for performance, knowing what's expected, and others that are fundamental to self-actualization and, in turn, happiness. I also believe that good managers encourage people, first, to build on their strengths and, at a distant second, to strengthen their weaknesses. To that latter point, I feel that we in business devote too much time and effort trying to fix what doesn't need to be fixed or can be improved only marginally.

"We also play the 'stick and carrot' game, if you'll excuse me for reversing the cliché. The stick in my mind is the here and now. Our pay scale is certainly competitive in our industry and geographic area. Bonuses can add an unlimited sum to any employee's base pay and are paid for performance of the individual, the team on which the individual works, and the company as a whole. Goals for performance are set by the individual and his or her boss, that boss's boss, and up the ladder so that we are all complementing and not duplicating each other and are all working toward the same result.

"The carrot is the future. Our 401(k) is generous; the company contributes 50 percent of employees' contributions of up to 6 percent of total pay. And every employee is given, at no cost, stock options that could lead to a hefty payday should we ever go public or if we are ever acquired or merged into a public company."

"A recurring theme throughout this book, one that you mention in your core purpose, is the need to create a fun environment. How do you go about creating one?"

"Fun to me is doing what I enjoy doing—I think that's a universal definition—and I want everyone here to do just that. I have a selfish reason, of course—I know that people who enjoy their working hours are more dedicated, enthusiastic, resourceful, and creative—all those good qualities that all managers look for in all employees.

"I hope I set an example in 2001 when I was CEO and knew I wasn't what the company needed in that job; I'm far more comfortable and competent working as a technology leader than across the company as a whole. I convinced our board to search for and hire a professional CEO. He has worked out very well, and I'm more focused on working with our engineers to improve our existing products and expand their applications.

"Changing jobs to be happier isn't exclusively for those at the top of the organization. Others in the company have taken similar paths, voluntarily stepping aside from 'more senior' positions to ones where they feel they can contribute more effectively and so create for themselves a more fun and rewarding environment."

"Aren't you talking about freedom here? The freedom to move within the company, to discuss hopes and aspirations with top managers and be heard?"

"Yes, and freedom doesn't stop there. We don't have a vacation policy, for example. Instead, we give 'off days'—18 of them for new employees, more for veterans. Employees can take them whenever they want and use them however they want—sick days, vacation days, whatever. Managers never need to wonder if an employee calling in sick, for example, really is; it's the employee's responsibility and choice."

"How would you summarize your success and the reasons for it?"

"We had three employees in 1987 when Vocollect got off the ground. We now have nearly 200 employees and will hire another 40 to 50 this year. We do more business in a week than we did all year only eight years ago and the pipeline for new business is full, even overflowing. Our employees and customers are loyal; people want to work here, and customers want to work with us. I just handed out pretty hefty bonus checks for last year. In short, we're enjoying our success; we're having fun.

"Why? Our core purpose and values are all about people. Getting that right lets every one of us focus all our energies on making our business successful."

7

THE AUTHOR AS GLOBAL CONGLOMERATE

Where make 'em smile is the reason for being.

I admit to being addicted to managing with Conscience simply because it has worked well.

I usually describe Geissler, Inc., of which I am president, as one-and-a-half people who are in the cerebral business, confusing everyone within earshot. In fact, my core business is writing speeches, articles, marketing stuff of all types, and strategies for businesses. What I do is very cerebral indeed since I help my clients think via writing. (Yes, one of the more important reasons to write is to cleanse thinking, a thought expressed years ago by any number of writers such as Henry Miller, who said, "Writing, like life itself, is a voyage of discovery.")

My corporation (a.k.a. me), on top of writing for business, is into teaching writing at the university graduate level and at companies and associations, turning out a book now and then, and occasionally behaving as an advertising/public relations agency and marketing consultant. So I am a miniconglomerate that operates under the umbrella of "words and thinking that work," and I am global, with clients, by way of clients in my headquarters city, in Europe and the Far East.

I developed and honed—in the most casual, informal, and serendipitous way imaginable—overarching "strategies" (really principles, or value systems) during my first few years in business. Each is founded on observations of similar businesses, some with dozens of employees and customers; I subconsciously separated what seems to work and what doesn't. My single criterion for "work" was subjective: employees and customers were enjoying themselves so much that they wanted to be together to help each other, the classic win-win that has been replaced too often by "I win, you lose." A correlation is that employees and customers stayed with the firm as if glued, and they smiled! I decided then and there that smiles are both the drivers and manifestations of success, and I wanted to surround myself with them.

I've used the words *casual, subjective,* and *serendipitous* for good reasons. I didn't decide consciously to observe other firms; I just did in the normal course of events, and I didn't decide that I needed a formal mission statement; I just created one in my head as I learned what works and doesn't. Many peers, competitors, and other entrepreneurs ask me how I've managed to stay and thrive in this turnstile business for more than 30 years. I tend to reply that I wish I had planned it, for then I would be The Master Planner of all time. But I didn't plan it in the classic sense, of course, and the big corporations I work with would laugh at my informal "planning process." Come to think of it, maybe they'd do themselves and others a big favor by emulating it. Regardless, serendipity and just plain good fortune played the biggest roles.

Anyway, the notion that smiles are the top line of my personal balance sheet and operating statement trickled down quite logically to my three strategies, all of which, again, are better described as "principles."

Stick to My Knitting

I confine my work to writing and teaching because I love it (just about every contributor to this book embraces "have fun" as a big reason for success), and I'm not distracted by "support" functions that I dislike and can't do well or quickly anyway. Doing so, of course, trades my billable hours for someone else's, a trade that I make gladly. So, as a first step, I retained a good and trustworthy accountant and put him in charge of *tracking* (*not* critiquing) my annual—never monthly or quarterly—income and outgo and filling out the countless forms demanded by the various levels of government with which corporations contend. I paid him a reasonable fee without qualms or grumbling.

My first accountant retired after being with me for 12 mutually beneficial years, surely not because the fees I paid him somehow made him rich. I retained another based on the first's recommendation, and he is still, almost 20 years later, happily toting my numbers and ensuring that I don't fall into the clutches of the IRS. Each has asked me once if I wouldn't be able to run my business better if I had a monthly operating statement. "Nope," I answered, "because I have a good feel of how well I'm doing financially, and a feel is good enough. I don't want to manage by the numbers or on a short-term string.

My second step to activate this strategy was to hire an assistant to, mainly, process the words I scribble on a lined tablet so that my clients can read them and to understand my business in enough detail to answer questions from clients when I'm not handy. My first assistant was experienced in the business and stayed with me for 18 years; my second, who knew nothing about the business but who is very bright and willing to learn, stayed with me for 11 years. Each left reluctantly to pursue other interests, and each left richer than they ever thought they'd be simply because of the third principle, below.

I'm for More Rapport

I keep customers who appreciate my talents, and, if perchance I get involved with those who don't or can't, I drop them as early in our relationship as possible, and as amicably. I am acutely sensitive about burning bridges.

Four individuals made up my customer "base": three are marketing or other managers of various divisions within large companies, and the fourth is a vice president of sales for a smaller firm. All are steady sources of work. A half-dozen or so other individuals became my "peripheral" customers; all can be counted on for sporadic orders.

All have been working with me for more than 25 years, regardless of corporate restructurings, new job functions and titles, moves to other companies, recessions, and booms. In this age of shifting loyalties, "why?" is a legitimate question.

My professionalism and talents enter into the answer, of course, as well as the fact that I am good at what I do, but that should be discounted quite severely. Here's why:

I can point to competitors who are also good writers and who struggle to retain clients and keep their doors open. So other factors enter into the picture, and the first is what I call the no-hassle job; I do not ask my client for more information, for example, until I have first exhausted all other sources. I do not ask for feedback on, say, first drafts when I am quite unsure about direction, content, or style (which is extremely rare if I have done my homework up front).

A second factor is to always look for ways to maximize my clients' investments in one assignment (e.g., a speech) by suggesting ways to use similar ideas and verbiage in another medium (e.g., a speech converted to an article or a press conference). One example: an article covering the design of a hull for a high-performance boat, published in a magazine read by engineers, was revised easily to fit a training program for the company's salespersons and distributors.

I read many years ago that it costs something like 10 times as much to find and develop a new customer as it does to keep one in the fold. (Ken Lovorn, in Chapter 9, says that it costs nothing to keep a customer if employees do their jobs. Jim Nairn in Chapter 4, agrees that 10 times more is pretty accurate.) I've come to think that 10 times is far too low an estimate; 50 or even 100 times seems far more realistic, so I go to heroic lengths to keep my customers in the corporate fold. Some examples: I lent a customer who was going through a divorce that temporarily tied up his assets the tuition for his son's college. I took charge of the funeral arrangements for another client when his father died and he became too distraught to function. I joined a golf club so clients could play either with or without me. I lent the money for a down payment on a home that one client wanted to buy, but, because of unusual circumstances, couldn't qualify for a mortgage. And so on.

These acts of friendship were the main reasons I became the busiest and most expensive writer of corporate gargle in town—at least that's what my clients said I was—and I jokingly said that I would move smoothly from 110 percent of capacity to 140 and hardly miss the sleep. I was, in truth, working myself to death, so I called a meeting with my Big Four to discuss how we could work together to smooth the ups and downs and level me off at a more reasonable pace. We decided on a system of communication within which I would signal them when I saw a downturn coming, and they would postpone or accelerate certain assignments to accommodate me. That I am still alive is proof enough that it all worked pretty well for years, and not one of my clients jumped my ship for another's.

But I think that there's a more important lesson to be learned: that rapport with clients works in all directions for the benefit of all. One client tells me often that he works with me because I am as interested in his success as I am in my own. Of course I am; his success means repeat business.

Share the Profits and Benefits with Employees and Customers

My formal profit-sharing plan for employees is extremely generous, and it's only one perk. I paid for the complete college education of my first assistant and for all sorts of computer-skills courses for my second. The corporation pays all costs for health insurance and copayments up to $50,000 and has made several interest-free loans to employees buying a home or car.

I am, as I write this, paying for the college education of my second assistant, and she has not worked steadily for me for several years. I'm doing this for both altruistic and selfish reasons: she is extremely intelligent and talented and I enjoy giving her the opportunity to develop her full potential. And I know that she compliments and thanks me to others whenever she can, and eventually that comes back in the form of psychic or financial rewards.

Customers share the profits—now, isn't *that* a novel idea—with free parking for baseball and football games (my home/office is near the stadiums), parties before and after the games, an invitation to the Geissler Invitational—billed as the world's most exclusive golf tournament since only 12 people are invited—and, perhaps most important for everyone concerned, a conference room for meetings not only with me, but also with their other suppliers. "Other suppliers" can include my competent and friendly competitors, and they—and my customers—ask regularly why I allow this apparent intrusion. The first reason is that I win: I love my good competitors; they stimulate and "grow" the market for our services and we all benefit. Besides, we often partner on the same projects. I dislike my bad competitors for the opposite reasons.

Everyone involved enjoys meeting at my place, where we can turn off the phones and other distractions such as unwanted visitors. No distractions equal a tighter focus on the project at hand, a higher level of creativity, and better "products," which of course translates to satisfied customers and repeat business.

And then there's the sheer comfort of it: my place is fully stocked with coffees, teas, nibbles, and the best booze in the city. Late-afternoon meetings that stretch into cocktail hour and, occasionally, a simple dinner, are the norm, and, because they are at my place, I don't waste time, billable time at that, driving to the desert wasteland of a corporate office. The costs of booze and food are so minuscule compared to the billable hours I gain that I don't even account for them. Everybody wins, even my clients, who get to leave their offices and imperious bosses for a legitimate reason.

The worst businessman I know is another writer of corporate information, and a pretty good one at that. Nevertheless, during his 20-plus years in the business he has lived from assignment to assignment, the nervous equivalent of living from paycheck to paycheck. One expensive consequence has been his continual search for new clients because, for several reasons and with few exceptions, he could not develop the rapport with clients that is necessary for repeat business. He met with me over lunch to ask me why.

"Well, you're a good writer, so your talent isn't the problem," I advised, and then told him about my bar, parties, golf games, and so on. His reply: "I can't afford to do all that."

"Let's see," I said. "You can afford the horrendous costs of sitting around between jobs and not billing your time while searching for new customers. But you can't afford the relative pittance of hospitality, friendliness, call it what you want."

He argued: "It would take a long time for my investment in hospitality to pay off." "True," I said, "at least six months." "I can't wait that long," he replied, and I could see that he was stuck in the self-defeating paradigm of short-term thinking that guarantees mediocrity and frustration, and that is described in Chapter 1. I gave up; he is still complaining years later that business is bad.

I asked two of my clients to comment on this chapter. "I recognize myself," they replied. One said that I should make a stronger case for my facilities. "I work with you to a great extent because we can really focus on the task at hand and let our creative juices flow when we meet there, away from the countless distractions of my offices." "I love our brainstorming sessions at your place," added the other, who meets here often with me and his designer, sometimes only with his designer.

Then, almost as an aside, one said that I was a pretty smooth writer too. Is the product less important than the ambiance surrounding it?

8

LESSONS LEARNED FROM LIFE ON A ROCKY ROAD

This small manufacturer of valves has survived on innovation and employee/customer satisfaction. It barely survived 15 years as a cash cow.

Dick Conley is director of engineering at Kerotest Manufacturing Company, a designer and maker of valves used by distributors of natural gas and other industries. He is highly respected by his peers and customers for his engineering savvy, and he has been employed by Kerotest for more than 30 years. He relates his experiences:

"I've learned a lot during my 30-plus years here that supports the premise of this book, and which I've revisited and formalized while contributing to it. Customers indeed shape our and every other business, and the overarching purpose of every business is a satisfied customer. Employees are needed who recognize these basic truths and serve (some say delight) customers beyond their expectations, and those same employees are willing to work their tails off to do that if they know the goals and share in the success of the company. I've also learned that all physical assets stem from customers, a concept I had not understood consciously before, and I wonder how many people in business do. Profits and the value of the business inevitably jump when we work toward those ends. It all seems so simple, yet it all seems so elusive.

"I'm pleased to say that Kerotest adheres to many of the principles. For example, every employee, and I do mean every, shares in the company's fortunes. We became an ESOP in 1985—after more than 15 years as a cash cow for a much larger company, a topic that I'll get into later—and everyone is given, at no cost, shares of stock as a yearly bonus. We don't have any outside owners. The value of a share is determined at the end of every calendar year by an independent auditor, and operating statements are posted every month for everyone to see. Our retirees all enjoy a nice nest egg.

"Our workplace encourages employee satisfaction, and, as a result, customer satisfaction. We don't tolerate discrimination or harassment of any type; we encourage teamwork and our managers are open to suggestions for improving product quality, lowering costs and delivery times, and increasing safety, which is a very big deal here. Managers are also open to suggestions for new products that we could or should develop and have a formal process for submitting and evaluating new product ideas. It's the idea that is evaluated, not the position of the submitter.

"Back to the workplace: We work in teams, and, as you'd expect, we encourage total quality management and continuous improvement. No one works on trivial tasks such as creating slogans or banners or unnecessary reports, and we make sure that everyone knows that he or she is critical to getting the job done.

"We don't play favorites, with reserved parking, for example, and everyone dresses in business casual. And, of course, salaries and benefits are competitive. That's fundamental.

"On a more personal note, I love my work as a designer and inventor of valves. I'm an engineer through and through, and management lets me be one without a lot of outside distractions.

"As for customer focus, point 1 in our contract with production workers is: Do what it takes to satisfy customers (no more 'it's not our job'). Point 2 is: Do it in a team environment (if you can't work as an effective team member, you can't work at Kerotest). Our administrative staff is acutely aware of these goals and works toward them as well."

"Survival in This Business Is One Measure of Success"

"We've been modestly successful throughout much of our 95-year history. (Survival alone is a measure of success, especially compared to many of our contemporary companies that no longer exist. Does anyone remember J&L Steel, the B&O, Hussey's, and many, many others?) We'll celebrate our centennial in 2009, which I suppose says that we must be doing many things right.

"Four years-long periods stand out as good examples of how employees and customers worked together closely for mutual satisfaction; I'll talk about them in chronological order.

"You could say that Kerotest, during the first half of the 20th century, was key to developing America's oil fields and the oil industry, and by extension the age of the automobile. The low pressure of oil from the first shallow wells could be contained by the cast-iron valves of the time. Then, as wells were drilled deeper into the earth, pressures increased and cast iron was just too weak for the job.

"Kerotest worked with the drillers to develop and test a cast steel valve that could handle the pressure. The valves were tested with kerosene under pressure, giving Kerotest its name. They quickly became the mainstay of the company's product line and the preferred valve in the oil fields, and held that position until World War II, when Kerotest was virtually taken over by the government and supplied countless valves for the war effort. In our absence, competitors took over the oil field market, and Kerotest could not regain its share. But the company survived.

"That innovative kerosene test led to another in the '60s, when the nuclear business was in full swing. Many valves in nuclear plants were leaking borated, radioactive water through their stem packing, raising the radioactivity in the plants to dangerously unhealthy levels, requiring very expensive clean-up efforts. An engineer with Westinghouse—the leading builder of the plants at the time—discovered somehow that we had developed a packless valve and called us in for a presentation. There was no question that our valves could stop the leaks, but could they handle the pressures, temperatures, and flows required? The higher pressure and temperatures requirements were satisfied, but flow capacity was another matter.

"An independent lab made a mistake and overrated the flow capacity of the Kerotest valve. Our principle competitor discovered this mistake in our advertising and brought this to the attention of Westinghouse. In fact, they went so far as to perform a demonstration flow comparison test. They designed and set up a test that consisted of two tanks holding the same amount of water, one drained by the competitors' valve, another by our packless design. The test proved what they suspected and we learned: our valves could not handle as large a flow, but they didn't leak. So Westinghouse and we questioned if the flow specifications were realistic; were such large flows really needed? Wouldn't a lower rate be acceptable?

"Engineers from Westinghouse and the predecessor to the Nuclear Regulatory Commission reviewed the data and decided that flow rates could be reduced without jeopardizing the operations or safety of the plants, and we landed huge orders for our valves for many years—until the nuclear business collapsed in the early '80s.

"That success story was the direct result of employees and customers working together to solve a very serious problem. Everybody won: We did with higher sales, and Westinghouse and its customer, the NRC, with safer plants. And we've never heard a complaint about flow capacity.

"Our involvement with the nuclear business surfaced again in 1980 when we bid on a government contract for 5000 valve sets to be installed in a huge uranium enrichment plant. Each set consisted of 13 precision valves, seven self-actuated valves—the expensive kinds—and they had to snap shut or open in milliseconds. Together, the sets represented many millions in sales, and, if we were the successful bidder, the contract would be the biggest order in our history. Fifty other companies bid against us, and some were heavyweights like Robertshaw, Lockheed, and Borg Warner . . . all much bigger by far than Kerotest and all with physical and people assets that we could only imagine.

"Our management committed to the project, I was named head of the development team, our CEO convinced us that we could be the winner, and our bankers agreed to finance the new plant we'd need.

"With that sort of confidence and commitment, we worked around the clock for a year, established a close rapport with the customer, built prototypes that passed all the tests, and won the contract for half the sets. We invested several millions in a building and the necessary equipment, hired 50 people at attractive wages, and, within a year, began to ship production units. We filled the entire order on schedule over five years, greatly increasing our revenues and profits.

"We survived the ensuing 15 years or so by serving our traditional markets, which eventually provided us with what we hope is our next big opportunity. During the past year we collaborated with our customers in the natural gas distribution business to design and manufacture a better, less expensive ball valve made of high-density polyethylene. The valves were designed using a new software program that allowed us to shave excess material without affecting pressure ratings. The result is a valve that is smaller, lighter, easier to install, and easier on customers' pocketbooks.

"The valves will be made at our plant in Louisiana, not overseas, where many competitors have moved production, saving good jobs for Americans. And the early enthusiasm for the valves expressed by gas distributors is now being expressed by water distributors and other industries. It's no wonder that our expectations for this product are high.

"The important point is that without the very close cooperation between our customers and designers, the valves would never have seen the light of day. We won with a new product line; our customers won with superior performance at a lower cost.

"Just this past month I was able to demonstrate again how customer involvement and satisfaction leads to sales. We are developing a new battery-powered electrofusion controller for use with polyethylene piping systems. After all sorts of internal debate about what customers want and are willing to pay for—two entirely separate questions and answers that enter into almost every purchasing decision—I met with a top engineer at our largest customer, a gas utility, and laid out the options. He was both surprised and delighted that we asked for his input (is it that unusual?) and influenced the design in ways that will surely broaden the marketability of the product. He promised to order more controllers from us and volunteered to spread the word to his peers at other utilities. In essence, he has become an important arm of our marketing department, and we're gearing up for a surge in orders."

Courting Disaster as a Cash Cow

"And now for the darker side. Back in the mid-'60s, Control Data Corporation (CDC), a maker of mainframe computers that was based in Minneapolis, bought Kerotest. The story of CDC's ownership demonstrates the opposing and negative mission of management, stockholder value.

"CDC bought Kerotest when it acquired Commercial Credit Corp. and they wanted to get into the business of making process control valves, an adjunct to their computer business. It was an OK idea (well ahead of its time), but it didn't work in practice simply because CDC's management was too focused on computers, which they figured would be the more profitable part of their business. So Kerotest, which in some years contributed 1 percent of sales and 10 percent of profits to CDC, was basically ignored. By that I mean that requests for capital were brushed aside, so naturally our plants soon bordered on obsolete, and our R&D efforts withered. Kerotest became the proverbial 'cash cow.' We fed money to the dying mainframe business, and stagnated.

"Not knowing what else to do with this strange business, CDC sold Kerotest back to its employees just at the tail end of the boom in nuclear plant construction, when Kerotest's profits were at their peak. The timing was great for CDC—but not great enough, apparently, because CDC went out of business soon after—and terrible for Kerotest, which borrowed heavily to pay for the overvalued stock. The value of the stock has risen over the years, but not anywhere near as fast as the Dow; we are not a glamorous business. Nevertheless, the stock is a wonderful perk for employees.

"The bottom line is simply this: When we are collaborating with customers to develop new products that solve problems or meet needs, we employees are satisfied and are happy to be working here. During these times, the company is quite profitable. When we lapse into that self-defeating paradigm of cost-cutting to be lean and mean, employees become fidgety and profits shrink. We have bounced back from several of those dismal times. The best course for management, our employees, and customers is, clearly, managing with Conscience for satisfaction. Our history proves it."

Dick philosophized a bit after telling me this story of his company: "Your book is needed—you've hit on a great topic—and it's timely. It seems that we reward the scoundrels of the business world, and the good guys toil in obscurity. That's not right. Another point: Our young people think that performance in business is graded A, B, C, D, just as they were graded in school. In fact, there are only two grades in business, or there should be: 100 percent and fail, and I know that 100 percent, perfection, isn't possible all the time but it sure can be the goal. Think of it this way: If the janitor cleaning the floor leaves a pile of debris in the center, the floor is still dirty. If the heart surgeon cleans two of three arteries doing a triple bypass, the patient isn't cured or could die. If we make a marginal valve, it will always be marginal. We don't need that."

9

I COULDN'T BELIEVE MY EARS!

A premium product at a palatable price yields phenomenal growth for this engineering firm.

Lovorn Engineering's founder, Ken Lovorn, explained how he formed and is growing his company: "I'll never forget it. I was in a meeting of about 20 top and middle managers of my former employer, an engineering and construction company that had been in business for about a century and employed 7000 people. The company's primary customer, the steel industry in North America, was on its well-known skids, and orders for design and construction had shriveled both in number and size.

"The steel industry is dead," pontificated the president. "Nevertheless, we will continue to aggressively pursue new business from this, our traditional market. In fact, we will step up our sales and marketing."

"I couldn't believe my ears. Surely this man was not so mired in the past—stuck in his outdated paradigm—that he didn't realize his own contradiction. Surely he knew that the dead cannot be resurrected. Surely he knew that new markets needed to be pursued and opened if the company was to survive.

"I couldn't believe my ears for the second time as the managers applauded in homage to their so-called leader with an ostrich complex. Could the power to hire and fire be that much more potent than the power of simple reason? Did our president surround himself with 'yes' people? I answered my own questions: Yes, and of course he did.

"I flashed back to an article that I had read recently: one of the 10 corporate sins that guarantee failure is 'fearing the boss more than the marketplace.' This company's managers practiced that sin to perfection. I also knew that all sorts of research concluded that smart employees privy to a reasonable amount of information—which we were and did—make better decisions than the smartest top executive. In this case, the 'smart' employees chose to sit on their tongues.

"The inevitable happened. A grand old name in engineering/construction went down the chute, and a grand new name, Lovorn Engineering, was born.

"I don't mean to imply that Lovorn Engineering was born because of my impulsive reaction to one event. Far from it, as my work history will confirm.

"I graduated, in 1970, from the University of Oklahoma with my degree in electrical engineering with special emphasis on logic circuit design. I immediately went with a design firm in Oklahoma City and was put in charge of the electricals of a three-million-square-foot office building. I figured I gained 25 years' experience in three years on that one project alone. Well, the company's workload dried up, so

I moved to another design firm, this one headquartered in New York City with an office in D.C., and then to an architectural/engineering firm in Alexandria, Virginia. When the controller with that firm resigned, I smelled something fishy, so I joined another firm, in Buffalo, and watched as my previous employer filed for bankruptcy.

"The owners of the firm in Buffalo didn't like my management style, whatever that very general comment means, and they never explained it so I guess they didn't know either. Truth be told, I didn't like their style either, especially when the top guy guaranteed me a bonus and then reneged without reason. It was then that I learned the importance of trust, of integrity in all relationships, including—especially—relationships with employees and, of course, customers.

"So I landed with the firm with the ostrich as president. During my 10 years there, I watched his management style, which boiled down to cutting costs despite jeopardizing the business's abilities to attract good employees and new customers with quality work. To be more specific, he would staff up when there was a big contract to work on, and lay off most of the worker bees—the designers, never the managers—when the workload was lower. And he set up a subsidiary in the Philippines to do the designs we did here in the States because costs per man hour were so low. What an illusion! Total costs actually rose when we in the States had to redo the shoddy designs produced by the overseas office, despite supervision by American designers sent there. I learned then that the folks putting lines on the paper or computer screen are key to the quality that customers expect and demand, and that cutting headcount can self-destruct the company.

"The result was an organization chart that looked more like a cylinder than a pyramid—there were almost as many managers as there were designers, and too many of the managers were cronies of the president and couldn't (wouldn't) be fired, giving respectability once again to the idea that hiring your friends can be destructive. And, as I've already noted, soon there were too few contracts to support the top-heavy structure.

"I somehow saw what was going on, and decided to get out from under managers bent on destruction of their companies and destruction of their employees' lives, and do my own thing. After all, I reasoned, I had learned a great deal about what creates success and what creates failure, and I knew the difference.

"I wrote a business plan with the help of some new software—remember, I needed that software because I had spent most of my career as a designer and midlevel manager of design teams, not as a manager responsible for the revenue and profits of an entire firm.

"Writing the plan forced me to define my core mission for the business: to provide a premium product at a palatable price, thereby creating a competitive advantage based on value. I can remember when 'competitive advantage' and 'value' were the buzzwords of business. As is the way of buzzwords, they were replaced by others invented by consultants bent on doing the same thing under a new rubric. I'm from the old school; I feel that competitive advantage and value are timeless.

Core Values, Not Magic, Yield Impressive Results

"I realized then, just as I realize now, that my mission isn't new, that just about every business is on a similar tack whether it is expressed explicitly or not. I also realized that implementing the mission is the tough part, especially since engineering has become pretty close to being a commodity. We in the business know how difficult it is to sell 'better' or 'premium' just as it's difficult to sell peas or paper clips as 'better.' Difficult, but possible. So I arrived at what I call my core principles, convinced that they are the keys to continuity, growth, and profitability of my business.

"First, avoid greed, espouse contentment. Many years ago I discovered the guns/butter curve for governments. It says, quite simply, that all societies must find their balance of spending on guns [defense] and social betterment [butter] that the citizens are willing to accept. If spending for either guns or butter exceeds some undefined limit, then spending for one or the other must decline [or taxes or deficits must rise]. Officials at the top must then decide who to satisfy, the generals or the citizens.

"A similar search for an acceptable balance faces managers, except that the two curves are labeled 'customers' and 'employees.' The question then becomes 'how much should be invested to satisfy either or each group?' The simple answer for me is: 'more than my competitors.' Satisfying both groups leads to competitive advantage and continuity of the business.

"Of course, something has to give when investing more, and the 'give' for me is profits and managers' compensation, which, in the case of a small company like mine, can be one and the same. What never gives is compensation and benefits for employees who do the real work.

"Explaining this simple concept to my peers usually prompts retorts along the lines of sending me to their favorite shrink. After all, they reason, the point of every business is to maximize profits, a kissin' cousin to that awful mantra that has brought down so many businesses: stockholder value. My critics are both right and wrong: right in that I am as interested in profits as anyone, and wrong in that I will content myself with lower profits in exchange for continuity of the business—which means that my employees and customers can go about their lives without fear of my disrupting them with a decision based on greed.

"*Second, strive for zero turnover of 'good' employees and customers,* good employees being those who understand and agree to work within my core values, and good customers being those who recognize the value we bring to their businesses. The corollary to this is to strive for zero expense for recruiting and sales, two of the biggest eroders of profits for any business.

"We're close to meeting those goals. Our customers stick with us; repeat business is 90 percent of our total. But, in a perfect example of how employees and customers are intertwined, after almost three years in business, I had to let one of our 20 engineers go largely because of his insensitivity to a customer's needs, another because he for some unknown reason developed some pretty lax work habits.

"I hired the first engineer based on his 15 years of solid experience, great references, and outstanding qualifications such as a professional engineer's license. I never asked his previous employers how he got along with customers. . . . I assumed he was OK there, and you know what the first three letters of 'assume' are.

"Anyway, I put this guy in charge of the electrical design for a small, three-story office building, and he overdesigned it big time. The electrical equipment rooms, one on each floor, were at least twice the size needed, raising the initial cost of the building and, more importantly, reducing the space available for rental. That would cost the customer several thousand dollars a year for however long he owned the building. Unacceptable.

"I trusted this engineer so much that I didn't check the design before he sent it to the customer. That's a strike against me, isn't it?

"The customer called a meeting with the three of us and pointed out the overdesign. I agreed. My engineer defended his design and refused to change it. I could hardly believe my ears, again. Neither could the customer: he was incensed, and had every right to be.

"So I redid the design myself within a crash schedule, costing my business thousands if you count the cost of the original and revised designs. The actual cost was probably much higher: my customer advocate and I had to spend considerable time smoothing the ruffled feathers of the customer. If there's any good news in this story, it's that the customer, an architect/engineer with whom we've worked for years, has forgiven our foibles and is still working with us.

"Which brings up a major point. I'm fond of saying that it costs nothing to keep a customer; all we have to do is the job we're contracted to do, and do it better than expected. We didn't do the job in this case, so the cost of keeping the customer was horrendous and unacceptable. Yet it was far lower—probably in the area of 10 percent—than the cost to create a customer from scratch.

"Are customers and employees my mother lode of assets? You bet. All my other assets—computers, desks, and so on—fall out from these two.

"I implement the two principles above with several actions:

1. Pay designers at least 5 percent above the going rate, and recognize excellence with an even higher premium and with awards such as company-paid dinners for the designer and his or her family.

2. Provide comfortable, people-friendly space for employees, which encourages creativity and efficiency. For example, lighting levels are high enough to discourage fatigue, low enough to minimize the costs of power. And I installed a thermostat to control the temperatures in our space. Did you know that a study of comfort in offices concluded that employees generally are satisfied with temperatures if they can control them?

3. Offer ownership in the company to all employees by way of a very generous profit-sharing plan. In that way, all employees have a stake in how the company is managed, a vested interest that ensures their continuing involvement in the continuity of their careers and the careers of all other employees. It also fosters teamwork at all levels of the company, which leads inevitably to higher customer satisfaction and repeat business.

4. Believe—really believe—Peter Drucker when he said that customers determine what a business is and behave accordingly by, first, giving each customer what I've come to call 'creative value'—solutions that go beyond what customers ask for or think they need. An example: The specifications for an emergency electricity generating system at a hospital called for two generators. I presented statistical and engineering evidence to administrators that the hospital would be protected against catastrophic power outages much better if three generators were installed, and that the additional cost would be very nominal. They agreed, thanked

me, and have rewarded our creativity with several contracts for other work.

Another example: We exceeded the expectations of a local bank on several projects so far that the bank's project managers actually revised our bid price upward on subsequent projects. They said we earned the premium. That's creative value at its best, and they are the kind of customer that recognizes and rewards it.

5. Retain one employee to be the 'customer advocate' in our office; ours owns 25 percent of the business, so he has a bigger financial stake than most employees in our drive to satisfy customers and grow the business. His first job is to know our customers so well that he can virtually read their minds so that our designs are shaped to match their needs as precisely as possible or to exceed their needs when appropriate. I jokingly say that our customer advocate can be our customer zealot; he sometimes takes his job too seriously, if that's possible. For example, not long ago he got so carried away with satisfying one customer that he extended payment terms, severely hurting our cash flow. I suppose that's a good news, bad news story.

"Has implementing my principles worked well for us? Consider that we've grown—as measured by the number of employees and revenue—by 2000 percent during the past three years. Ninety percent of our business is repeat, and employee turnover during the company's formative years has been only 5 percent and is expected to be nil as we mature and continue to grow, albeit at a slower rate."

I first called Ken Lovorn and asked him to contribute to this book after I read about him in the "People to Watch" column in the local paper. I found a man of extraordinary compassion; a man who had adopted five young Russian orphans after traveling to Russia and somehow maneuvering through the maze of bureaucratic muck needed to give these children a better life. He told me that, statistically, two of his children are alive because he adopted them; about 40 percent of orphans in Russia die before their 21st birthday. By itself, it's a story of a life well spent. I think that his display of compassion has spilled over to his business, but he demurs. "I did nothing special," he'll tell you. I don't believe it. Do you?

10

BEFORE AND AFTER: THE TAWDRY CLASH OF MANAGEMENT STYLES

Managing with Conscience   Managing for Stockholder Value

*From the calm of employee and customer allegiance
for 33 years to the chaos of headcount reduction
and customer desertions in one easy acquisition.*

X is an entrepreneur who prefers to remain anonymous because, "The folks who bought my business will not hesitate to rattle my cage if I say anything to defame them." Suffice it to say that he is a successful businessman living in a small town in California. At age 71, he is convinced that "to retire is to expire" and that he'll "probably be back in the saddle soon." He is also convinced that many managers today "just don't get it," with "it" referring to the need for continuity based on managing with Conscience.

X is in a clash—a war, if you prefer—of management ideologies that ignited when he sold his successful company to a huge conglomerate after its managers promised, at the bargaining table, to continue X's style of managing for the satisfaction of his triangle of employees, customers, and suppliers. The acquirers then decided, just after the final papers were signed, that they didn't really mean it. He spoke to me about his colorful experiences, particularly that deceit and its results:

"My style worked very well: absolutely no layoffs for the entire 33 years that I was in business. I know and like my employees and their families, visited the plants regularly to chat and find out how their lives were going. Layoffs of strangers are distasteful; layoffs of friends are repugnant. Management by walking around, I think the folks who wrote *In Search of Excellence* called it, and I was doing it long before the book came out.

"If we lost a customer I can't remember who or when. We surely never lost one of the 70 customers that provided us with 80 percent of our business. Maybe we lost one or two of the other 5000 that provided us with the rest; I don't know. Regardless, we came very close to zero turnover of both employees and customers, and reveled and prospered in its lower costs. We were reasonably profitable, even when the general economy was down. If we weren't, why would that conglomerate want to buy us?"

Lean IS Mean

"But—the buyers are so deluded, so arrogant, so sure that they have a lock on good management—that their first act when they took over was to change management styles to 'bottom line' or 'lean and mean' mania. Of course, that destroyed the culture I had spent most of my life building.

"The results, after only a few months of them at the helm, haven't been pretty. Sales have slumped as customers became aware that the close relationships they had with employees were no longer possible. They're buying from other companies with which they can at least have a chance of restoring those relationships. Heads—their terrible term that dehumanizes people by reducing them to heads without bodies or names—have been cut across the board, justified as cost-cutting that is necessary to 'save' the company, which everyone involved knows is bull; it's symptomatic of the short-term thinking that is so endemic with those who cannibalize a good business.

"The person who was president—a close friend of mine—couldn't live with the new climate of contention and resigned in a huff. He was replaced by an accountant who knows nothing about the business or the people who operate it, but everything about the numbers; there is a clear and important distinction between the two, and every manager with a scintilla of sense knows it. Other employees have told me that they are looking for a way to escape what they perceive to be a ship sinking with the overbearing weight of misguided decisions made by greedy managers. They no longer can see the secure and comfortable future that was once so clear and comforting.

"The number and ferocity of customer complaints are surging, and nobody's there to answer them. Even today, months after I sold the business, I'm getting calls from friends (customers) who are tearing their hair out in frustration. Quotes are now taking weeks to prepare instead of two to four hours. Shipments from stock now take one to three weeks, when they once took only 24 hours. Why? Too few service people, policy changes, computer 'updates' that extend the time needed to process orders (but supposedly lower the cost) but shorten the time needed to prepare a report for management. Can you believe it? Slower order processing and shipments, faster reporting of irrelevant financial data. Lord, who comes first?

"Now, faster than a speeding bullet, these misguided souls can get reports that show how many customers and how much business they've lost—all valuable information for those looking to justify even more self-destructive cost-cutting and headcount reduction. Idiocy.

"Managers are so busy cutting jobs and other costs that they can't respond, so they pass complaints off to lower-level employees. They call it 'delegating'—a BS term they learned at some MBA school with a fixation on numbers—which means that they don't want to hear the bad news themselves, a clear validation of how far removed they are from the actual day-to-day operations of the business. Then they're surprised when complaining customers complain even more.

"None of this type of decimation happens overnight, which head-counting and cost-cutting managers can't seem to understand. The raping of a company like mine—and I suppose any other—is like a cancer growing so slowly that it's not obvious to the managers who haven't a clue about the business's potential. Lost sales are dismissed for all the wrong reasons—the 'buyer quit,' or 'the customer is loaded with inventory and isn't placing new orders,' or 'the bad weather has killed production.' They never look at the real cause—their own vision and management style that are tilted in the wrong directions—so they never notice that the sky is falling. Sunbeam is a good example."

The Massive Concept Labeled "Relationships"

"The vast difference between them and me is wrapped in one massive concept: relationships and how they're built, maintained, and nurtured. To me, 'relationships' is the hook, the competitive advantage that allows entrepreneurs to succeed in this big tough world. As long as the Enrons and Tycos of the world don't understand that—and I for one don't think they ever will, with their heads stuck so solidly in the sands of numbers—there will always be room for people like me.

"Let me dig deeper. When I talk about relationships, I mean the close bonds to that triangle of employees, customers, and suppliers. By adding suppliers to the mix I'm intentionally broadening the focus of this book, unless you think of suppliers as employees, as I do. Like employees, good suppliers work for the success and continuity of the company. I haven't laid off a good supplier in years either.

"One reason that those in the triangle have endured is that I do not believe in secrets; everybody involved knows anything they want to know about the business, and, maybe, a lot that they don't care about. I never BS'd them: no secrets or lies, ever. Try that on a CEO of a giant company!

"Loyalty is another key. I've always stuck with those who brought me to the dance. I really believe that cliché and live it with everybody in my triangle. I'm sure that if I take care of my triangle, sales and profits will take care of themselves, starting with sales. It's easier to push down from the top line of the operating statement than it is to push up from the bottom. My business has proven the truth in that: sales and profits have grown in lockstep at respectable rates, certainly faster than the industry we're in as a whole. All that has happened without a sales force; all of our business is repeat or from word-of-mouth from customer to customer and often from supplier to customer. Isn't that another way of saying customer satisfaction?"

The Two Paths Open to Managers

"I see managers today as taking one of two ideological routes. The first is to focus on people skills, customer satisfaction, product integrity, and profits that are 'reasonable,' which I think of as 'sufficient to sustain' the business. The second is cost-cutting, staff reduction, benefits squeezing, and the like.

"I'm convinced that good managers will take the first path if they want to succeed over the longer term. It encourages creativity and strategic thinking, maximizes sales by raising customer acceptance levels, and elevates the capabilities of employees. None of that has anything to do with the second path, which is the one chosen by bad managers who intend to cannibalize the company. They prepare the company for acquisition by spinning the books to the best light, and the light stays lit for only a short time. In my value system, that's lying and cheating, and, over the long term, it inevitably leads to catastrophic drops in sales and profits, and soon the entire business goes down the drain and all sorts of lives are unnecessarily disrupted or destroyed.

"The list of corporate rapes seems to lengthen every day—and the managers responsible for them get the headlines that they don't want but they sure as hell deserve. Top managers line their own pockets and the troops are left with empty pockets and futures. Good managers avoid that kind of blatant chicanery."

11

IF MANAGERS ONLY KNEW OR CARED: BROKEN COMPANIES, BROKEN LIVES

*The incessant and insane drive for higher profits
and stock prices has sacrificed countless lives.
Meet a few here.*

The Enron, WorldCom, Global Crossing, Kmart, Polaroid, Arthur Andersen, Qwest, and other debacles proved that regular employees, those who carry out the strategies of the higher-ups, lose the most when a company fails. They lose their jobs, pensions, savings plans, and those stock options that executives promised would be their wealth of the future. Senior executives, directors, the big shareholders who are positioned to see the debacle coming—many escape with their wealth intact and lucrative pensions or jobs handed to them by the old-boy network. Only a few find their way to jail.

The angst of lower-level employees is palpable. Most, if not all, felt that they had jobs for life, as they were told at their entrance interviews, and they lived accordingly; that is, they saved little for the future simply because rock-solid companies and pensions/savings plans promised that the future would be both secure and comfortable.

While the notion of a job for life is considered terribly naïve these days, it wasn't back in the '50s, '60s, and '70s, when these people were hired; in fact it was a "selling point" to come on board. Westinghouse, for example, had existed for about a century, and the company's primary business—the generation, transmission, distribution, and use of electricity—is so fundamental to our society that it was hardly imaginable that the company would not continue ad infinitum. In addition, Westinghouse had survived several serious close calls[1] and disastrous management failures that put the company on the brink of bankruptcy, and that fact alone "proved" the company's resiliency and staying power. In fact, it proved that managers are not immune to greed and arrogance and that the company could withstand only so many lapses in judgment.

A confession. I fell into the "resiliency trap" and paid for it dearly, if not disastrously. During the early '90s I was in a meeting of the company's financial gurus, and the subject of the credit arm's bad loans came up. The opinion of one highly regarded attendee was that the losses are "far more serious than top managers are admitting in public," which of course is the way they protected their jobs and stock options, at least temporarily. I had lived through a similar crisis—similar in that "bankruptcy" was bandied about—in the '70s and could not believe that this "crisis" would not be resolved and become just another bump in our fat, dumb, and happy road.

A few days after the meeting I reconsidered and talked to a respected competitor. "I'm diversifying," she said. "Westinghouse could very well be history, and soon." I believe in serendipity, and that conversation was enough to get me moving, albeit slowly, toward diversification of my client base. I opened negotiations for additional business with two other companies for which I was working sporadically and, during the following two years, contracts from them grew from about 10 to 40 percent of my revenues. When Westinghouse toppled, my revenue dropped by more than half, pretty traumatic but manageable for my small business, and far more palatable than a plunge to zero.

Pittsburgh and surrounding towns (and dozens of similar towns throughout the United States in which Westinghouse had built plants) suffered greatly with Westinghouse's decline. At its peak, Westinghouse employed almost 20,000 in the Pittsburgh metropolitan area, 2000 at its headquarters in downtown Pittsburgh. A rule of thumb is that every job in manufacturing creates three support jobs: doctors, lawyers, restaurant and government workers, writers like me, and so on. So some 60,000 people in western Pennsylvania—a huge part of the population—depended, at least in part, on Westinghouse for their livelihoods.

Many of these people took jobs in other areas; others duked it out with declining job opportunities and took "any old job" to stay in their hometown. The population of the city itself shrunk by almost half because of Westinghouse and other reasons, as did its tax base. As I write this, the city is "distressed," an official classification that is equivalent to being on the cusp of bankruptcy. Its bonds are close to junk, its political leaders under attack, its downtown decaying as retailers and other businesses either close or move to the suburbs.

A frequent topic of conversation among those who are still here starts with, "Just think of how much better off the city would be if Westinghouse had survived." Or, "If only Westinghouse had survived, just think of how our lives would be better." We express similar thoughts about the steel industry, but we seem more willing to justify its shrinking as one effect of globalization, not mismanagement.

The former CEO I mentioned in the Preface rationalized that Westinghouse had contributed greatly to the city. Yes, of course it did, during the century or so that it was a viable company. It also contributed to society as a whole on a global scale, and we should, and do, applaud that. However, Westinghouse also contributed greatly to the decline of a once-proud city, and no amount of self-delusion or appreciation for the past can erase that simple fact.

The angst of employees as they dropped, singly and in groups, from the corporate tree was bolstered by a powerful disillusionment. They had believed that managers actually work for the continuance of the company, not—I am not being too harsh here—to line their pockets. "Greed at the top" became a major topic of discussion in meetings and, mostly, in less formal gatherings at bars and restaurants. Tempers flared, voices raised, lawsuits threatened, too many drinks were downed.

The damage, like a rampaging cancer, spread to homes. Spouses saw their lifestyles and dreams for the future shattered; some took to the bottle, others to the divorce courts. Children were told to forget Harvard, think community college or trade school or work after graduating from high school. The health of many deteriorated, as expected when stress soars and depression takes over. Some died from the stress.

How many jobs and careers were lost, lives disrupted, families hurt, homes sold or repossessed, educations sidetracked or foregone, stockholders broken? How many Great American Dreams had turned to Great American Nightmares? Several million is not an exaggeration. Following are several from my small circle. I've changed their names to protect their privacy.

Carl graduated in 1967 from Carnegie Mellon University—when CMU was still Carnegie Tech—and the next day joined Westinghouse in the company's well-regarded management training program. His studies focused on fine arts, and he was quick to draw people, buildings, bridges, whatever, and the drawings showed a flair for reality with a touch of the mystery that comes with an appreciation of Mary Cassatt and the other great impressionists.

The human resources person told Carl at his entrance interview that he would have a job for as long as he wanted it in the company's marketing communications group, where his talents could be used most effectively. All he had to do was display reasonable diligence and skill, which everybody knew was no great shakes for a graduate from a prestigious university like Tech, and to behave with the highest integrity and morals; Westinghouse employees were a fun-loving group, but the line was drawn at a few drinks and golf games.

Eighteen months of training at six divisions at six locations landed Carl back in headquarters. The sign on his desk and his business card said "communications manager," and he set out to be one.

Life was good for the next 25 years: raises were bestowed on him steadily, reviews by bosses were consistently stellar, respect from peers and suppliers was unwavering. Nobody could blame Carl for feeling pretty comfortable with the straw in life that he had drawn. He supported his wives (yes, he stumbled his way through three) and his one daughter, and he indulged his loves of midsized cars, upscale golf, and top-shelf scotch for his Rob Roys. To his discredit, he lived on the edge of financial meltdown, but so what? He believed it when the HR person said he had a job for life, his pension was secure, and he was riding high as a respected, even favored, employee.

Little did he know (how could he?) that he was living a dream, and the dream was set in a house of cards called managing for stockholder value.

Yes, Westinghouse went from paternalistic—an awful term for actually caring about the welfare of employees and customers—to caring more for the bottom line. The result was a series of bad management decisions related to a subsidiary's risky investments in real estate, followed by frantic spin-offs of healthy businesses to cover the losses, and then bankruptcy and a merger of the few remaining assets with CBS.

Carl lost his job when the division he was working for was sold, in management's mad dash to cook the books, to another company. He became "redundant" at age 48. He tried freelancing as a communications manager for a few years before realizing that he is a corporate animal in need of the structure and discipline of a larger organization.

He invested the little money he had saved in a concentrated job search aided by a top consultant. After six months of frantic but focused effort accompanied by extreme angst, he landed a job with a Westinghouse spinoff as the communications manager in the team marketing a new brand of products. "The best job I've ever had," he said often, "because my bosses let me be creative."

Sales and profits for his product line soared, and Carl's reviews were outstanding. He was named marketer of the year—only a few years before he was terminated again, this time at age 62.

The decision to terminate him was one of those perversities that can only be attributed to management's devotion to the bottom line.

Carl's product line, about 15 percent of the company's revenues and an even higher percentage of its profits, was booming, but the remainder of the business was struggling. So top management cut headcount "across the board" rather than selectively or, preferably, not at all if management could muster any faith in the future. The cuts came only a few months after the general manager declared that employees are "our most important assets."

As I write this, Carl is struggling to maintain his sense of worth and his naturally jovial nature as he searches, for the second time in 10 years, for a job that uses his considerable experience and talent.

During his 20 years with Westinghouse, Sam rose to creative director of the advertising group, in charge of investing a multimillion-dollar budget to enhance the sales, profits, and image of the company.

When the company fell on hard times, the advertising budget was one of the first to be cut, in increments at first and then to zero. Sam became redundant and unemployed. "Best thing that could have happened to me," he said in a macho display of frustration for management. "Now I can get a job with a company that actually appreciates the strategic value of communicating with its many publics, and my talents to do so."

It turned out that being downsized wasn't the best thing for Sam after all. As he looked for that dream job and then any job at all in his field, he realized that his age, 50, was a liability. "Too many companies are convinced that the young bucks own the great ideas," he'd say. His position high on the corporate ladder, and his salary, were also preventing him from getting a good job; he heard "overqualified" in many rejections, despite his willingness to start at a lower position and pay. He also complained that he was "tarred by the Westinghouse brush of failure," despite not having any direct part in it. "Who wants an ex-Westinghouse employee?" he'd ask.

He started to drink more heavily than ever, and his marriage, already shaky, finally fell apart. The bank foreclosed on his house, and he and his wife moved to separate, small apartments. His two children were denied the educations they had counted on and Sam had promised; Sam had graduated from a prestigious and very expensive liberal arts college and expected his children to follow in his footsteps. His daughter settled for a few selected courses at the local branch of a community college, and his son went to work as a server in a chain restaurant after graduating from high school. Disillusioned and disgruntled by the destruction of his dreams for the future, he, like his father, fell into the bottle.

Sam's life deteriorated in lockstep with the duration of his unemployment. His anger at the corporate world and its insensitivities to the plights of its employees became manifested in such declarations as, "Employees are commodities like peas, to be chewed and spit out," and, "Employees are disposable, cattle to be exploited for the benefit of management," and, "Top managers who behave like those at Westinghouse should be in jail. They lived off us when we worked for them, and now we're broke and they're enjoying huge pensions and bonuses as some kind of 'reward' for destroying a household name."

After several years of living by himself and fruitless search for employment, Sam bought, for future royalties, the recipe for a pet food, and then arranged for interim financing. As of this writing, the pet food is beginning to sell in quantities so modest that revenues cannot meet his living expenses or the expectations of investors. He is living in a small apartment, trading rent for minor repairs to other apartments owned by the same landlord, and he talks regularly of suicide, and when his friends suggest counseling, he rejects it as "fraudulent."

The consensus of many of his friends is that Sam will never recover from losing his job at Westinghouse, but we hope we are wrong. We remember his creativity fondly and deplore that it is now wasted. We also think that his former wife and at least one of his two children, will never recover from the disruption of their lives.

Other friends are convinced that Sam is at fault for his situation and that he blames Westinghouse too loudly; after all, many people lose their jobs and find others. They say that Sam's struggles stem from his bitterness and self-pity, which of course stems from his humiliation at being fired.

Regardless, at least four people are living lives that are far less fulfilling than what they envisioned, and management's failures were the triggering events.

"I'm a two-time victim of stockholder value," said Jim, a former vice president of marketing for a smaller manufacturer of electrical equipment used in commercial buildings and homes. Now in his late 50s, Jim had been searching for a job for almost a year after being let go the second time, and he was feeling the financial and emotional pain, as were his wife and two daughters, both of whom were attending a prestigious and expensive university.

"My first encounter was probably the less dramatic or traumatic. I directed the integration of a smaller company into a much larger one, which involved, among other things, combining two sales forces and replacing one nameplate with another. Please understand, the sole purpose of doing this was to cut costs by cutting employees at the expense of customer satisfaction. Convincing salespeople and customers that this was OK wasn't easy, especially when I was convinced that it was a bad business decision.

"Regardless, when the integration was complete, I was dispensable and was 'let go,' as were hundreds of others."

Pete, your author, responds: "I wrote a speech for your president about that time. He wanted to convey his strategic vision to employees and had scheduled a series of meetings around the country. I realized at our first meeting that what he really wanted to do was present a glowing financial plan. When I pointed out that he ignored such important considerations as opportunities for employees to grow into new management positions and opportunities for customers to expand their business with the firm, he gave me that blank thousand-mile stare. I honestly think he didn't listen to or understand a word I said, and he presented his financial projections to very bored audiences. I know; I attended some of the meetings and watched as the attendees fidgeted."

Jim continued: "Yes, the president was following the corporate line that profits are everything, and the way to profits is to cut costs, mainly people costs. But, Pete, in a perfect example of what you call the 'prima donna paradigm,'[2] he'd take the corporate jet when a commercial flight would have been just as quick and convenient. He didn't cut the costs of his privileged position, and many employees saw the hypocrisy of that. I know I did.

"Anyway, I was unemployed for about six months before I landed at a huge company that had acquired a number of Westinghouse businesses and merged them into their own. I started out as a product marketing manager and then was promoted to a new position in strategic business development. When I took that job, I was told it was 'permanent.'

"The company, which was honored only a few years earlier as one of the best-managed in the world, pigged out on risk, as you say. Debt rose to unconscionable levels, and the stock rose in lockstep. The parallels with Enron and Westinghouse are too close to miss.

"It was déjà vu all over again. As costs rose, mainly for servicing debt, cutting costs became the objective of management, and here I am, a year later, still looking for a job. Many of the top guys at the company, by the way, are either still at the top or living off their generous pensions. And smaller stockholders are licking the wounds of a 50 percent drop in the value of their holdings.

"My wife is now working to cover at least some of our expenses, and we are paying for others, including the educations of our daughters, with savings that we thought would be our retirement. We're thinking of selling our house, and we've become very careful about our so-called discretionary spending. The bottom line is that we've changed the way we live, and we can see more changes in the future."

Jack is a vice president of a nationwide consulting firm that specializes in outplacement of managers and professionals.

"Our business has changed dramatically over the past few years, and much of the change is the result of businesses cutting costs to raise profits, and their general disdain for employees. Severance packages have shrunk. For example, released employees were, only a year or so ago, given an average of six months of our services; now they're given three to four months. The irony is that more time is needed these days to negotiate a new job. I find cutbacks like that to be just another example of the insensitivity to the human condition that is endemic with too many managers. Another example that I find even harder to live with is the sad reality that only 15 percent of our corporate clients bother to contact us to ask how their former employees are doing. They've forgotten the very people who were once their 'most valuable assets,' which is, of course, just another example of hypocrisy at the top.

"Dozens of people walk in here in various degrees of shock, disillusionment, and anger; almost all have been 'downsized' or 'rightsized' by companies looking to cut expenses to raise profits and stock prices. They've been hit by that relentlessly insane drive for a continuous string of higher profits.

"The extent of their psychological damage varies all over the lot. A few are quietly resigned to the situation; sometimes their angst bursts through their calm exteriors as the tensions of getting a new job increase. Most, however, are boiling mad and their self-esteem is badly shaken. A big part of my job is to work with them to get back to their normal emotional state, which can take months, even years.

"A former corporate counsel was probably the most angry client I have ever handled. He was mature, in his late 50s, vigorous, in great health, at the top of his game. He had worked for the same company for almost 30 years, his entire working life, and he rose to be the top attorney. He lived the good life with his wife, two kids, a home in a leafy suburb, and a secure future.

"Then the CEO of his company decided to cut costs everywhere, to become 'lean and mean,' and heads rolled and damn the human consequences. The law department was reorganized and most of the work farmed out to a local firm. As a result, my client's position was no longer needed at that firm.

"My client left with a year's pay and a bellyful of bad feelings. He needed another job with a corporation—he didn't have the experience or temperament for a job with an outside firm. Well, his timing was unfortunate: corporations were shrinking or dying in the area, but the law firms were expanding and doing just fine. He and his family were enmeshed in the social fabric of their neighborhood and the city, and, initially, moving to another city was not an option. However, after about six months of fruitless searching, he decided to consider other locations—over his wife's very vociferous objections.

"Desperate by this time, he accepted a job in a much smaller city, and it turned out to be a big mistake. After only a month or so on the job, he realized that he didn't fit the culture of the company or the city, and he became increasingly uncomfortable. He lost much of his self-esteem again, sure that he could not even be trusted to decide on something as simple as the right job, and his wife, back in his home city, wasn't much help in restoring his emotional center. She tried, but her unhappiness at the prospect of moving showed despite her best efforts to hide it.

"The bottom line is that this man died of a heart attack in his motel room in the city that he had hoped would be his new home. His wife is totally convinced that the stress of a job that didn't fit his nature, added to stress of looking for employment, killed him. She could very well be right."

Jack then switched to his own story: "In hindsight, I was one of the more fortunate victims of managing for stockholder value. I landed on my feet after two episodes, one divorce, the alienation of my daughter, and the cusp of bankruptcy. Sounds like more of a daytime soap than a life, but that's what happened.

"I was the vice president, human resources, for a large regional financial organization, living a pretty idyllic life in a small city, when one of the behemoths of the industry made the handful of owners an offer they couldn't refuse, a.k.a. big bucks. The acquirer offered me a senior HR job in its headquarters, a job with far broader responsibilities than I had, and, not seeing a good alternative, I accepted. Mistake #1. I guess you could say that the move was a step up in responsibilities and pay, but a huge drop down in compatibility. My new employer was addicted to the bottom line, and I never could accept that management style; no wonder I became unhappy, edgy, and angry.

"So, a few years later I quit and accepted another HR job, this time with an old-line, closely held manufacturer with the highest reputation for quality with its employees and customers. Maybe I was trying to replicate my happier, earlier experience. It turned out to be Mistake #2. I admit to several errors of judgment that people tend to make when they are really ticked off, as I was. These days, as a career management consultant, I advise my clients to be aware of this. I was also charmed by the president and majority owner of the company and thought so often that 'I want to work for this guy' that I forgot to see the bigger picture.

"The company was sold a few months later, for big bucks again, to what I graciously call a 'band of corporate thieves and rapists.' I knew I wouldn't fit when the new president said to me: 'The only way to track employees is to put deer tags in their ears.' I couldn't believe his lack of compassion and respect.

"As you'd expect, the company was pillaged—its better businesses sold to line the pockets of the new owners—and was soon half the size it was when I joined it. Hundreds of employees, some with 30 years of valuable, hard-to-find experience and knowledge in a very specialized business, were let go; the company decimated its most important assets, its seed corn, and its future. The value of people wasn't considered. It was a cesspool of alligators, this disdain for people and for the continuity of the business. Customers fled the sinking ship.

"I was among those cut. 'You've done a great job; you're just not part of our team,' I was told was the reason. What a farce! I can't to this day accept or understand that kind of rationalizing—it reminds me too much of government when one party takes over from the other and people are let go because of their party affiliation, not their abilities or contributions.

"Here I was, in my 40s and angrier, more fearful, more anxious than ever, depressed and convinced that I could not make even the simplest decisions and be sure that they were right. I was angry at myself, my former employers who had betrayed me, and all of corporate America for its ethical lapses.

"I took my anger out on my family and friends simply because they were handy. Big Mistake #3, and the inevitable happened: my wife and I divorced, my daughter 'left' me at the very vulnerable age of 10, and my finances tanked. Angrier than ever, I made my next bad decision and started a consulting business with my few remaining funds and a partner. Mistake #4. We did OK for a few years, before my partner dropped out and our biggest client left because of a long strike. I tried and failed to breathe life into the business with too little cash and a couple of remaining employees. I almost lost my house, and my financials were a disaster.

"Now, late in my career, I love my job and my new wife, and, after some 15 years of alienation, my daughter and I are getting along just fine. With all that, I suppose that I am one of the luckier victims of management greed, but. . . ."

Mary, a chief psychiatric nurse at a large mental health hospital, has "seen it all." By "all" she means the devastating mental and physical damage heaped on workers who have lost their jobs and on their families who feel the reverberations. The damage seems especially severe if the reasons for unemployment were management's malfeasance. "They seem better able to understand their plights if they lost their jobs because of a downturn in the economy, for example, maybe because such causes are acts of God and they've lived through a few. They are confused, betrayed, and enraged when they feel that bad management was the cause."

Mary specializes in rehabilitating people with emotional illnesses brought on by severe trauma. "I've seen literally hundreds of patients who have been traumatized by being downsized, to use the cliché of the day. Most of my patients are men; women seem better able to cope with the loss of a job. And many of them are skilled, blue-collar, unionized workers who expect the company to value their expertise and the union to protect their rights and wages.

"The trauma typically brings on or exacerbates four problems: drinking, divorce, disease—both mental and physical—and debt. The four 'Deadly Ds.'

"I live in a small town outside of Pittsburgh in which Westinghouse was by far the major employer. The Westinghouse plant employed several thousands, many the second and third generations of families that depended on the company for their livelihoods. They were fiercely loyal to the company and figured that the company was equally loyal to them.

"Not so. As everyone knows by now, Westinghouse disappeared for what they perceive to be the wrong reasons, and workers' loyalty and security turned to bitterness and hate, anger and despair.

"A case in point: A close friend of mine was married to a second-generation plant worker who lost his job in the late '80s, when he was only 45 years old. This man, who had spent years developing and honing his well-paid skills, lived for his job and the respect it gave him. When he lost his job, he lost his self-respect and his ego support. Always a 'loner,' he became more introverted than ever, and, finally, in despair, he took a job washing windows at pay and skill levels far below what he was used to. He became depressed and started to drink heavily to relieve the symptoms, making him even more depressed in that never-ending circle of self-delusion and destruction. He became edgy, then downright nasty as he became more drunk. He and his wife fought over trivial matters, and he was often physically abusive.

"The wife took a job for the first time in her life, opening a whole new and friendlier world for her. She urged her husband to get psychiatric help, but he was too proud for that. She finally left him and found a new place to live.

"I suppose the good news is that he survived two serious heart attacks and, at 60, is working at another menial job. His wife is struggling to make ends meet. Two of their four children dropped out of a public college, and one is a confirmed alcoholic at age 26. Not a pretty picture, but maybe prettier than the plight of a family that I'll call the Smiths.

"Mr. Smith lost his job at a glass plant nearby, and, as he became more and more angry about it, he also became more and more of an abusive drunk. He drank at home, at his social club, at friends' homes—anywhere he could get his hands on booze. Drinking led to petty arguments with his wife, which escalated and broadened to slugfests with his wife and family. One day he almost choked his teenage daughter to death. The wife feared for her and her daughter's lives, and her daughter escaped to a friend's house.

"It's so easy to get drunk in this town, where it seems that every other doorway on Main Street is a dirt bar that has become a social club for the disenfranchised. When they were employed, the men would stop at one bar or another for a relaxing beer on the way home. Now that they don't have anything to do, they just stop anytime of the day at a favorite bar to drink and grouse about their lot in life and to fritter away the few dollars left from their savings and small pensions. It's all so destructive.

"Visibly drunk a good part of the day, Mr. Smith couldn't hold even a menial assembly line job. Nobody—except maybe Mr. Smith himself—was surprised when he came down with severe problems with his pancreas, which some folks around here called poetic justice. His doctor told him to quit drinking or be dead in six weeks. He stopped for a week or two, and then went back into the bottle as deeply as ever. I guess he didn't figure he had anything left to live for. Isn't that a form of slow suicide? We're waiting for him to die as I'm telling his story.

"Mrs. Smith found a job that paid the bills and little else, and then left to live in her own apartment. She now works two jobs and is recovering from what is commonly called a 'nervous breakdown.' Her credit card debt has put her on the cusp of bankruptcy.

"Drinking, divorce, disease, and debt. All might have happened without unemployment; there's no way to know, but the unemployment was the trigger, wasn't it?

Another patient of mine was 'involuntarily retired'—the big boys call it attrition in some misguided attempt at humanity—in his late 40s from a U.S. Steel plant, and he was convinced that his life was over. Angry, depressed, and disillusioned, he took to the bottle, a familiar escape route by now. He'd stay up all night watching TV and drinking to the point of senseless oblivion.

"After a year or so of this destructive behavior, his live-in girl-friend kicked him out of the house, and he tried to commit suicide, which got him automatically committed—it's the law—to the hospital where I work. After three weeks of group therapy—which, uncharacteristically, he accepted wholeheartedly—he realized he was in trouble and reversed his destructive behavior by cutting his drinking back to the occasional beer and his self-pity to a quiet confidence.

"The good news is that he bounced back to his former self, his girlfriend welcomed him back into their house, and he's working steadily."

12

THE COMMON THREADS

Managing
with Conscience
for
Competitive
Advantage

Contributors to this book share many values,
strategies, and tactics that contribute to success.

Management is, first and foremost, about people. When managers talk about common culture, shared vision, continuous learning, customer satisfaction—you know the basketful of buzzwords—they are talking about people, and I see a three-way tie for the three groups vying for the title of "most important." Employees, of course, because all these concepts pertain to them, including customer satisfaction; customers, because they are the reason for the organization; and then the people in the background, surely the largest group: families, friends, suppliers, and businesspeople supplying ancillary services.

Contributors to this book have tilted their management style strongly toward Conscience (a.k.a. people) in the following ways. Perhaps, if you agree with the tilt, your challenge is to incorporate their insights into your style and mission.

Employees

1. Hiring (attracting the right talent)
   –Candidates understand the culture of customer satisfaction and how it affects their behavior and continuity of the business.

2. Retaining (job satisfaction)
   –Stretch capabilities, creativity, innovation.
   –Set reasonable (not outlandish) limits/goals.
   –Measure performance by customer satisfaction/retention.
   –Compensate above average; include profit sharing and other incentives and offer ownership.
   –Encourage continuous learning by remembering always that customers buy knowledge, whether directly or as part of products.

3. Firing (always rare in an organization managed with Conscience)
   –Insensitivity to customers' needs.
   –Drop-off in performance.

Customers

1. Finding/soliciting (attracting the right organizations)
   –Almost all from referrals from existing customers

2. Retaining (satisfying those in the fold)
   –Listen always to needs and wants.
   –Give more than expected.
   –Anticipate changing needs/wants.

–Adjust services and products with time and changing conditions.
–Rewrite those murky instruction manuals.

3. Firing (always rare)
   –Outside cultural boundaries

Measurements

Regardless of style, management must be accountable for performance, but "performance" is a big word, a large abstraction that most managers try to reduce to quantifiables. "If can't be measured, it can't be managed" has been an enduring and popular aphorism for years.

Companies that are managed with Conscience measure performance by using different yardsticks than companies managed for Stock. Here are the yardsticks, in order of importance.

1. Employee turnover[1]
   –High (up to 20 percent) for the first six to eight weeks after hiring, nil thereafter

2. Customer turnover
   –Close to zero; 100 percent retention of "good" customers (those that understand and appreciate the company)

3. Sales expense
   –Close to zero; satisfied customers are the best sales force by becoming advocates

4. Recruiting expense
   –Close to zero; commensurate with growth of revenues

5. ROI/profitability
   –Above industry average; a result of 1–4

Guiding Principles/Values

1. Listen to employees, customers, and suppliers; understand, respect, and empathize.

2. Act with integrity at all times; do the "right" thing. Be truthful in communications.

3. Enjoy; fun on the job is key to productivity, performance, and customer satisfaction.

EPILOGUE AND PROLOGUE: THE IMPLIED CONTRACT THAT BINDS BUSINESS AND ITS PARTNERS

An invisible contract based on a shared purpose connects employers, employees, customers, suppliers, and communities. The nature of the contract is a critical management choice.

More than two centuries ago, Scottish economist Adam Smith posited that everyone acts always in his or her own self-interest. Very few people today would deny the truth or relevance of that observation. Many of us, however, would add a caveat: that self-interest demands a balancing of the many and varied motives (the self-interests) of all the people who rely on business for their ways of life. Finding a balance that is workable in perpetuity (the endless life of a business that is granted by government) is the privilege of management and dictates management "style." In addition, "all the people" includes all those who participate in the business most directly and are, therefore, most affected by its actions: employees, customers, suppliers, and the citizens of communities in which the business operates, that is, every business's partners.

The implied contract among partners recognizes and deals with their varied motives; it actually governs the "tilt" or "style" of management. We've already seen how the tilt to managing for stockholder value can ruin businesses and lives. Managers who slavishly adhere to that tilt (or to any tilt, for that matter; balance is the name of the game) risk the enormous financial and social costs of loss of business or the business itself, litigation, resentment, reducing whole communities to empty shells, destroying or disrupting millions of lives, and so on.

We've also seen how choosing a tilt that is more respectful of the human dimensions of business can be tremendously rewarding in many ways, and for all partners.

The Essence of the Contract

Countless people have legitimately defined "management" and its main focus to suit the tenor of the moment; most focus inwardly on the organization.

The focus of this book and the purpose of management came up at a dinner party recently, and comments illustrated the inwardness of managers. The president and owner of a marketing research firm said that the only purpose of a business is profit, perhaps the most internally focused and simplistic purpose of management that is conceivable, and certainly the antithesis of the focus of this book. A middle manager in a large company pointed out that a few years ago a popular rationale for management was to provide meaningful employment, which, while broader than profits and a step in the right direction, is still too narrow and a bit socialistic or unreasonably altruistic. Others pointed to companies that are managed for quality, productivity, efficiency via reengineering, safety of employees, and many others that zero in tightly on the organization.

Few definitions seem to see management as a "system" within which every partner or participant lives, preferably comfortably, happily, productively, profitably, and synergistically. This broader definition—broader in the sense that it transcends the boundaries of the organization—is founded on the notion that all partners share a single overarching purpose for the organization. That purpose can be summed as *continuity* (decisions are made that link long-term strategies with short-term actions and that help ensure that the business lives in perpetuity). It is supported and made possible by *cooperation and reciprocity* (a feeling that we are all in this together and act win-win at all times) and by *communication* (a willingness to express viewpoints candidly and openly).

All partners owe it to one another, equally, to make decisions and take actions that reinforce that purpose, requiring that the contract be administered by *empathy*—that rare human skill that allows one person to enter another's mind and thinking. Empathy based on a deeper understanding of the shared purpose can remove the adversarial encounters that seem so prevalent. To cite just one of many examples that is based solely on newspaper reports, union officials often make demands that appear to be designed to destroy or damage a business (or a city). In response, managers seem bent on destroying the business and its partners—and the union—by threatening to move where costs are less. Yet, employees at every level should be most concerned and interested in continuity.

A second requirement is *compromise,* which is reflected in decisions and actions that balance economic and other interests, in turn requiring trust and reciprocity (if I bend, I expect that you will too) and mutual respect (I respect your position, and I expect you to respect mine). In other words, compromise weighs/balances pragmatism and idealism.

All partners must agree to a workable definition of *"success"* that rewards behaviors that lead to long-term viability, including the growth of revenue, profits, and employment that opens new opportunities for all partners and that supports the viability of communities.

And all partners must share a sense of *obligation and loyalty* that recognizes that the valued contributions of all partners in the past will continue in the future as long as value continues to be added. The medical profession is grappling with such an issue with its testing of drugs on humans in countries where restrictions are less stringent than they are in the United States. Are the companies that sponsor the testing obligated to provide the drugs—or complete medical care—to the persons tested for life? Free? For an "affordable" price?

Managers face similar issues. Assuming the people involved in the following scenarios are ethical, ask: Would a pharmaceutical company—or pharmacist—knowingly dispense a drug that could harm a customer? Would a manufacturer knowingly release a product that is unsafe? Would a financial planner recommend investments that are not suitable for a client? Before saying "of course not," add to the end of each question: even if, by not doing so, the negative financial consequences were severe? Is finding an answer more complex? Have the answers changed?

To be a bit more specific concerning obligations: Employers are obligated to manage prudently, in ways that do not jeopardize the viability of the business; employees and suppliers are obligated to increase their value to employers and themselves through continuous learning; and citizens are obligated to elect officials who advocate tax and other policies that are equitable in that they do not punish business, and, therefore, themselves.

Here is a modest call to action that, admittedly, is an attempt to start partners talking constructively and arriving at their own solutions. First, put the blame for a business failure where it belongs most often: on top managers who are approved by boards who are elected by shareholders. Therefore, executives, board members, and shareholders are ultimately responsible for failures, and they should be held responsible for cleaning up the carnage they cause.

Second, prudent managers can prepare for an unlikely but possible future by creating trust/transition funds (preferably in cooperation with enlightened governments) that pay for training of employees should layoffs be necessary. For example, a portion of the profits from outsourcing jobs can be used to train displaced employees or to supplement communities' tax revenues for a specified but extended duration, say a year or longer. Local governments, suppliers, and unions could start similar funds.

The pervasive ideal among contributors to this book is that human capital is the driver of financial success, not the byproduct, and, as a result, human capital must be nurtured with education, training, motivation, recognition, and much more that can, in my mind, translate to basic human decency. The subservient ideal is that contributors live by the implied contract with all their partners.

The contributors aren't alone. Costco's chairman, president, and CEO said: "We think when you take care of your customer and your employees, your shareholders are going to be rewarded in the long run. . . . I care about the stock price. But we're not going to do something for the sake of one quarter that's going to destroy the fabric of our company and what we stand for."[1]

Another believer is Caterpillar Tractor, whose chairman states in the 2003 annual report: "This is a company that knows financial results aren't all that matters. Developing, rewarding, and motivating people to ever-higher levels of achievement is just as important . . . and integral to our *continuing* success" (emphasis mine). The chairman also said: "I truly believe there are many great companies out there . . . organizations with integrity, ideas, and positive impact on our world. . . ."

He'll find a few in this book.

REFERENCES

"Living Large In The Corner Office," *Business Week,* February 23, 2004, p. 47.

Cassidy, John, "The Greed Cycle," *New Yorker,* September 23, 2002.

"Why Companies Fail," *Fortune,* May 27, 2002.

Kaplan, Robert S., and David P. Norton, "Measuring the Strategic Readiness of Intangible Assets," *Harvard Business Review,* February 2004.

Pittsburgh Tribune-Review, January 11, 2004, p. 67.

"Survey Finds Profit Pressure Leading to Poor Decisions," *New York Times,* February 7, 2004.

"The Only Company Wal-Mart Fears," *Fortune,* November 24, 2003, p. 158.

"We're More Productive. Who Gets the Money?" *New York Times,* April 5, 2004, p. A25.

Chapter 1

1. *The New York Times* of April 5, 2004, p. A25, reported in an article titled "We're More Productive. Who Gets the Money?" that, "American workers have been remarkably productive in recent years, but they are getting fewer and fewer of the benefits . . . workers have gotten little more than the back of the hand from employers who have pocketed an unprecedented share of the cash from the burst of economic growth."

    Business Week of February 23, 2004, echoes the *Times:* "CEOs are raking it in again, even as boards keep a closer eye on performance."

    Jim Browne of Allegheny Financial, in Chapter 2, asked me to write a chapter or book on the disproportionate rewards of being a high-level executive, evidence in his view of disdain at the top for employees especially, but of customers, too. I declined, reasoning that the book focuses on the positive results of managing with a more humane and empathetic attitude toward people.

Chapter 2

1. In the parlance of this company, "planning" encompasses setting the direction and focus of investing, the actual placing of funds, tracking performance, and adjusting the asset mix as conditions change over time.

Chapter 11

1. Westinghouse's finances were severely strained during the 1950s and 1960s by a series of antitrust violations and during the 1970s by long-term contracts to supply uranium fuel to utilities at unfavorable prices. Both crises were, clearly, egregious failures of management driven by growth and profits.
2. The "prima donna paradigm" is reflected in the arrogant behaviors by top managers for which lower-level employees would be fired in a flash. It absolutely guarantees that employees are furious, and stockholders would be too if they knew. Examples would fill another book.

Chapter 12

1. Turnover of all jobs in the United States is about 25 percent a year. All contributors to this book report 1 percent or less.

Epilogue and Prologue

1. "The Only Company Wal-Mart Fears," *Fortune*, November 24, 2003, p. 158.

INDEX